THE HOTEL REVENUE BIBLE

by Bruce Jordan

the Michael Jordan of Hotels (Author)

Contributing Authors

Craig Carbonniere, Jr
Deborah Gardner
Doug Kennedy
Halee Whiting
Calvin Tikokee

ISBNs:
979-8-9899889-0-7 (paperback)
979-8-9899889-1-4 (hardcover)
979-8-9899889-2-1 (eBook)
979-8-9899889-3-8 (audiobook)

Library of Congress Control Number: 2024901750

Published by

BAJ Publishing and Media LLC

Dedication

This book is dedicated to my mom, Lizzie, a strong woman who had to be strong not because she wanted to, but because she had to be strong for her children. She was able to raise three head-strong kids by herself. Most importantly, my mom made childhood miracles happen at Christmas when our financial situation promised otherwise! Mom, I love you 1,000 Reese's Pieces much.

Contents

Prefix

Revenue is one of the things that everyone needs, but few have the time or desire to master. Most of us are so busy being victims of expenses, that we don't know how to prepare our hotel to receive the revenue that we need and deserve. Therefore 98% of our time and energy goes on expenses and only 2% of our focus goes toward increasing revenue and getting the income that we need to move our hotel forward. The problem is that when I started out, I was on the opposite side of the fence where most of you are today. As an expense expert just like everyone else, I thought I didn't have the time, and I couldn't see the light at the end of the tunnel to get the revenue I needed and I was at least 10 years into my career. I found out the "problem" was 9 times out of 10 not expenses because whether I charge $100 for a room, or $200 for a room, usually my expenses were the same, but my percentages were lower because my ADR, of course, was higher.

Now I realize most of the problems we have in our hotel when it comes to finances are revenue issues. They're not expense issues at all. In this book, we're going to teach you how to master hotel revenue and how to maximize your hotel budget to keep those numbers rising.

You're going to learn about revenue management, social media, social media marketing, social media ads, food & beverage sales (F&B), food & beverage marketing, front desk sales and so much more to help you take your hotel revenues to the next level.

The number one reason most hotels fail isn't
because they don't know how to win, it's because
they don't know why they are losing.
Bruce Jordan Michael Jordan of Hotels (author)

Introduction

In this book you will learn things that you never knew about or even considered as an option to increase your revenue numbers. In the hotel business everyone wants to teach you operations. Don't get me wrong, operations are very important and great operations keep the guests coming back. But it won't necessarily get them in the door. As hotel leaders we spend most of our career learning or managing front desk, housekeeping, maintenance, and F&B. These things are nothing but ingredients in a pie. We spend all this time learning how to make tasty pies and little to no time learning how to sell them. And just like any other item with an expiration date, if we don't sell them in time, they will expire.

That's what happens to our hotel rooms ... we spend so much time making the beds and getting the rooms ready, no one sees the occupancy going down, rates going down, and in turn, revenues going down. Why? Because no one is focused on revenue. Most people in our business believe that if we just work hard enough at cleaning and delivering better customer service to a guest, the revenue will automatically appear like magic. Sadly, this is not true. If you watched my show *Hotel Management Do's*

3

and Don'ts, you would see how I dissect a hotel's operations and revenues without looking at one STR report. I don't know their financials or day to day systems for their operations. But with little to no information I can state the strengths and weaknesses and how to capitalize on them.

Today not only will you learn those skills and abilities times 10, but you'll also learn all the secrets to keep those revenues flowing and growing with little to no effort after you pump up your skill level. My All-Star Revenue team and I have put together the ultimate and greatest hotel revenue generating book the hotel industry has ever read. Come join us as we share our most sacred revenue tips and tricks that will have you slam dunking over your competition. Anyone can be number one with guests face to face, but after you read this book, you'll be ready to be number one at the bank!

Understanding Hotel Revenue Management

I started out in this business as an idiot. I started
out in this business as an expense junkie.
Bruce Jordan the Michael Jordan of Hotels (author)

They say what you focus on, you get more of. And 98% or more people in the hotel industry are focused on costs and customer interaction, which is probably why our expenses have increased drastically since the 1980s. Because it's all we're focused on. The thing they don't understand is that most issues hotels have aren't expense issues, they're revenue issues. And this is what I didn't understand. When I first started off my career in the hotel industry, it was in the accounting department. I was an expense cutting master. I never saw an expense that I couldn't cut. And that was my biggest mistake.

It was only when I understood how revenue is generated, how revenue is maintained, how revenue is saved … only then did I understand that revenue heals all wounds. As my revenue increased, my expenses decreased. I could cut all the expenses in the world, but I could never cut enough expenses to offset a huge loss in revenue. Until I learned the secrets that my team will be sharing with you in this book. If revenue is the problem, how come we're always focused on expenses? This book was designed to help you increase your revenue dramatically. This book was designed to help you see the other side of the field, the side of the fence that matters the most because you can have the greatest operation in the world, but if no one comes through the front door, it's all for naught.

This book is designed to help you get more business in the door then keep that business and keep more new business coming in. This is why we believe mastering revenue generation is like a religion. Revenue will give your hotel the many blessings you need. And this is the Hotel Revenue Bible.

Revenue Management

By Bruce Jordan

Know Your Customer

K nowing your customer - everybody thinks that revenue management is about setting rates and getting reservations. But the first step you need to learn when you're learning revenue management and setting rates is to know your customer. There are four types of customers that we must pay attention to in the hotel industry. Most importantly, these four types of customers are going to help us understand our position and the role that we play inside our industry and in our market segment. The first one of our four customer types is the bargain customer, the bargain customer is looking for a bargain, they need the lowest rate possible for a reason. To give you an example of a bargain customer, someone from the construction industry gets paid a per diem for their hard work. They're given a daily amount to spend, a set amount each day for their hotel and for their food. Everything else comes out of their pocket, which means it comes out of their paycheck. So they have to get the lowest rate possible. When you have to stretch that per diem to cover food and board, luxury is not an option.

The next customer is a value customer. The value customer is very different from the bargain customer, the value customer is also looking for a deal. But the quality of the hotel means something to them, it's not the most important thing on the list, but there has to be some quality involved. In addition, the value customer won't just stay anywhere. They won't stay at a hotel with a one-point review score, but they will stay at a decent hotel that has some of the amenities that most hotels offer, for instance, free breakfast. A value customer sees a hotel that has free breakfast as a value because they don't have to pay extra for the breakfast. Value customers are the second type of customers in our market.

The next type of customer is a quality seeker. A quality customer may not necessarily be looking for a great deal because they believe the amount you pay is what you weigh. In other words, a quality customer believes they must pay for quality, they don't want to stay in a place that is going to cause them problems. If you offer a quality customer a low price, they're going to think something is wrong with your hotel. Price is very important to a quality customer. Let me stress this … if the price is too low, the quality customer is going to believe your hotel is lower quality.

Finally, we have the luxury customer. The luxury customer wants the finest of everything. They want the best. They believe that they deserve more. The most important thing about the luxury customer is that they don't want to be surrounded by a bunch of bargain customers or a bunch of value customers. They want to be surrounded by people like them. They want to be surrounded by people that believe that $400, $500, $600 or on past $1,000 a night isn't a high price. It's a regular price for the luxury customer for the services that they are receiving. I'm going to say that again. From $400 to over $1,000.00 dollars a night is a normal price for a luxury customer because they believe in the value that they're receiving for the price they're paying, and it ensures them they are surrounded by others like them.

So, the first thing you need to know is your position in the industry. Once you have identified your position you now know the type of customer you want. You need to set your rates according to that position and the role that you play inside your specific market segment.

Understanding the Art of Rate Psychology

Now let's talk about setting your rates. The most common problem I see with people setting a rate is they don't use the Michael Jordan of Hotel's #1 rule and that's make your rates look appealing. You may be wondering how I make my rates look appealing. What are you talking about Bruce?

Your rates must look appealing to your guests. And the #1 way to make your rates look appealing to guests is by using numbers they're already familiar with. Your rate can be higher than your competition. And many guests will still book with you. It boils down to one or two reasons. One, the location is where they want to be and/or two, the numbers are talking to them subconsciously.

If there's something that's familiar about the numbers that they like, even though it's higher, they will feel the rate is sexy. To make your rate look sexy, you must use numbers that people are already familiar with numbers like:

11:11

13

99

10-4

7-11

7

69

Let's break it down! Funny but true: 69 is a number that guests identify as giving them pleasure. It's very popular around Valentine's Day. **Rate Example** – 69, 169, 269, 369, etc.

Seven is a number that guests identify as being lucky. Rate Example – 77, 177, 277, etc.

11:11 is a number that guests identify as being spiritual. Rate Example – 111, 1,111, etc.

10-4 is a military term and used on walkie talkies to mean understood. Rate Example – 104, 401

7-11 this number is popular in the U.S. because it's a franchise. Rate Example – 117, 711

99 is a number most people see everywhere. Rate example – 99, 199, 299.

13 don't use this number on Friday the 13th. Rate Example -113, 131, 213. Taylor Swift fans love this number.

123 is the first set of numbers we learn as kids. Rate Example – 123

101 means beginning or understanding. Rate Example - 101

These are just a quick sample of tricks you can use. Try to focus on numbers that guests see all the time or numbers that are popular in your market.

The next thing you need to do is you have to use the Bruce Jordan 49-cent rule. Back in the day OTA website used to display the whole rate on the websites. So, if it was $150.05 per night, the website would read $150.05 with the cents added. But today, to save data and bandwidth, most websites only display the main numbers without the cents. So a potential guest is not seeing the five cents, or the 15 cents, or any cents, the guest is only seeing $150 and this is what happens ... in today's market the website rounds the room rate up, it doesn't round down; so beware if you are setting a price to show familiar numbers it won't round down but will leave just the core amount. If I have a rate of $181.07, the guest sees $181. If I have a rate of $180.51, the guest sees $182. No matter what the penny amount is, a possible guest isn't going to see it until they get to the checkout screen. So, with the 49 cent rule, we round the rate up all the way up to nearest 49 cents. Let me give you an example.

If my system is producing a rate of $81.51, I'm already going to round up my rate to $82.49. The reason why is because the website is going to round up the rate anyway, the guest is not going to see $81.51, they're going to see $82. By rounding my rate all the way up to the nearest 49 cents, the guest is still agreeing to the same rate of $82. The guests don't see the rate until the checkout screen. And I've never had anyone cancel a reservation at checkout because it was rounded up to 49 cents. This is the issue. When you don't round up to the nearest .49 you're losing money. So why not take the extra dollar or the extra 90 cents and get the additional revenue? Why not get an additional 50 cents to 90 cents per night? If you have 55,000 room nights and you're getting an additional 99 cents for each booking, you just got an additional $54,450 by rounding up to the nearest 49 cents. That is the Bruce Jordan 49 cent rule. Always round up to the nearest 49 cents to capitalize off the website's removal of the change. Create your own Keep the Change program.

Hotel Listing

Listen, the most powerful asset your hotel has is its listing. The listing is the most underutilized asset by most hotel properties. They just don't get it. The worst thing you can do is throw up any old pictures, say any old thing, or type a telephone number & address and hope for the best. Your hotel listing is not the number two revenue generator, it's the number one revenue generator for your hotel property. Pay just a little less attention to the rates you set and more to your listings. In the hotel industry, we don't look at our listings enough and don't compare them to other properties and/or competition.

That's why a lot of people don't get the profits they hope for. First let's tackle the pictures. I always hear people say *I got great pictures. I'm good.* No, you're **not** good. Because all you have is just pictures of the hotel. Like I said before, that guest is coming to your room for a reason. Find out what they're coming there for and take pictures of that (or those) and put it inside your listing. If possible, make sure you geotag the pictures in your listing. What is a geotag? A geotag is an electronic tag that assigns a geographical location to a photograph, video, or a posting on social media. The reason why is that you need your guests to identify your location with the Things To Do that you should be taking a picture of. It is the reason why they're coming to your town, city or county. I'm going to say this again. You identified your hotel with the thing that they're coming there to do.

Their reason for coming is 50% of the sale. So make sure you not only have good photos of your property, your lobbies, your pools, and everything else, but make sure you have photos of the reason why they're coming there. Are they coming in to go to a park or are they coming to go to a stadium for a concert? Whatever they're coming for, you want to have photos of that in your listing.

Upgrades

Okay, the next thing to polish up is your property description. The next mistake I see people make in the property description is they don't put in enough details about upgrades that are available, they just think upgrades sell themselves. Upgrades don't sell themselves. I've never seen 50 guests a day walk through the front door and say, "Hey I want to pay more money." Which is why these things need to be inside your property description. Two, most managers don't put enough details about what a guest may be looking for. Here is an example: you don't say we have breakfast. You say we have a hot breakfast which includes eggs, bacon, biscuits (we have cereals that includes this type of variety). This is how you're going to know if a guest likes what you have or not. Give the guest as much detail as possible or as many letters as the listing hosting agency allows you to give so that you're able to sway a potential guest in your direction to lock in a sale.

Amenities

Next you need to list plenty of information about your amenities. Amenities are why a lot of guests choose a hotel. It can be the difference between your guests choosing your competition and choosing you. Every hotel has a bed. I'm going to repeat that again, every hotel has a bed. It's the other things inside of the rooms that the hotel may not have, like you, which may win you a new customer. You may have a hotel that has a smart TV with Netflix, YouTube, so on and so forth. Some of the other hotels in your market segment may not have them. The new smart TVs you just installed could give you the cutting edge over the competition. I see this happening a lot. Many hotels just have basic cable. *Your* hotel has amazing smart TVs, maybe a 55-inch screen TV in your premium rooms. When you're listing the things that you have inside your rooms, guests are thinking as they're reading *hmm that other hotel I stayed at last time, didn't have smart TVs. The other hotel I stayed at last time I was there, the TV was too small, I hated it. At that other hotel, I couldn't watch Netflix, I couldn't see my shows, I couldn't watch YouTube, I didn't have anything to distract my kids but the local stations.* So, list your amenities in detail, it makes a very big difference.

Location

People often have a difficult time talking about their location. When you're describing where your hotel is, you always want to use the smallest number. For instance, I just read a listing that said something like this: "my hotel is 15 miles away from a certain destination, which is about a 35 to 45-minute drive." I'm not going to say that I'm 35 minutes away, I'm going to say I'm 15 miles away. Because the number is smaller. When it comes to distance, most people digest smaller numbers easier. The other reason why I go with the smallest number is because I don't know what the drive is going to be. I can say that I'm 35 minutes away, and there could be no traffic or the driver speeds up and ended up getting there in 10 minutes. On the other hand, I can say I'm 35 minutes away and there's traffic and next thing you know, it takes them an hour and a half to get to your hotel. You always want to use the smallest number so that the guests can see the exact location.

You can even use blocks. For instance, if you're only two to three blocks away, I would not use smaller miles. I would say "our hotel is only three blocks away from this destination." Guests see blocks as something that's walkable. They think, "It's a block away. I can walk there, and that means I'm close to the location." Therefore, pay attention to which number you use as you are describing your location.

Things to Do

All hotel websites should list things to do in the area. Include the hours of operations for those attractions. For instance, if they're coming to you for Six Flags or they're coming for Disneyland or another theme park, include how many blocks from that attraction you are. Add the hours of operations, for instance from 10am to 10pm. Now your guest can make proper plans to check in and get the most of their day faster, which makes them happier. Those are the things that you want to focus on when you are building your listing. Focus on details that guests want to know and want to see and need more information about. Putting all the information they need on your page keeps them from clicking away from your listing and lets them focus on booking with you.

The other reason why you want to put this information in there is because it helps with your SEO (search engine optimization). SEO helps with how search engines rank your hotel's website. Guests will be able to find you much faster if the hotel's website is ranking higher. Another thing you want to pay attention to in your listing is if you accept pets. A lot of people are looking for pet friendly hotels, they're very hard to find. If this is an amenity you offer, be sure to list it and any details that deal with extra fees or regulations you may have.

Digital Assets

A majority of your hotel's business is driven through digital assets. What I mean by that is driven through your website and OTAs like booking. com, Expedia, Agoda and or other platforms for digital marketing like social media or search engines like Google. Through your marketing, your social media and other listings, people will see your hotel on a screen before they even think of walking through the front door. Many times, their buying decisions are going to be made on what they see from a digital platform (from a digital perspective). Online presence is extremely important when it comes to revenue management.

If potential clients can't make it past your website's first page, they're not going to book. They're certainly not going to book if they don't even see you online. No one will book a hotel they can't see. Your listing is the number one key to opening the door to unlimited revenue potential. After you understand your position in the market, you must work on your hotel listing.

SEO

You need great SEO. You need to describe your hotel in detail, including things to do and some of the landmarks in the nearby area. In addition to setting up your room types, you need to make sure that your room types are very descriptive and very active. The first thing I do when I'm working to write the copy (sales script) for a hotel website is that I look at the competition's guest reviews. I see why guests are staying there, I see why guests are complaining about the other hotels in that area. I identify a common problem amongst other hotels in that area, I put that inside of my listing to show that we don't have that issue at this hotel. If I see most guest are complaining about slow internet speed in my competition reviews, I'll add my internet speed in my listing.

The main reason I do this is to improve SEO, yes, we are back to search engine optimization. A guest that is tired of staying in hotels that have slow internet issues is going to search for "hotels in Los Angles with fast high-speed internet." I want to make sure I am using the keywords (words a person searching may use) so the search engines display my hotel to this guest on their first page of results. If I am the only hotel that has the "high-speed internet" keyword in their listing when the guest submits this search I will automatically be the first hotel the guest will see when they submit their search. There could be other hotels that have faster internet than I do, but since they failed to add that keyword to their listing, I will automatically outrank them. This is the power of SEO.

So, focus on your listing first, make sure your room types are described accurately, make sure you have enough detail inside your description to keep possible guests looking, reading and interested, and put in as much detail as you possibly can. The more research a person is doing on your hotel online, the more they're trying to convince themselves that this is the hotel for them. They're trying to make a logical decision with an emotional connection. Let me repeat that again, the guest is trying to make a logical decision with an emotional connection. Think about a time you stayed at a hotel and it looked great online. But soon as you walked in the door, it was nothing like what you had seen online. The price they saw online, that's the logical decision part. What the room looks like based off their past experience at other hotels … that's the emotional connection part. They're trying to make a logical decision with an emotional connection, and they only have a digital platform to use to try to make this connection.

Why Guests Choose Your Hotel

There are three main reasons why a guest will choose your hotel. Number one is location, that's one major key performance indicator (KPI). Nobody is going to try to stay at a hotel in the middle of the desert. So, location, of course, is most important. If they're coming to that location, they have a reason to be there, and you need to find out why they're coming and what's bringing them there.

Number two is going to be the rate, the rate plays a key factor in them choosing your hotel because they want to make sure they're getting what they pay for. People work very hard for their money. They want to make the most of it. With that being said, you have to make sure the rates you set are going to be comparable to what they're willing to pay.

And number three is going to be your review score. Your review score pretty much states the level of service or the quality your hotel has displayed to previous guests. These are going to be the main key KPIs that you should factor into your strategy.

Let me give you an example. Know what is going on in your location: there is a major concert coming to your area. Your hotel is 2-3 minutes away from the concert. Does this make your rate go up? Or does this make your rate go down? Usually this will make your rate go up. You can capitalize off the increased demand this concert will bring to your market. If you usually charge $150 per night, or $200 per night, because this concert is coming into town, now you can increase your rate to $400 or $500 per night. Why?

Because the demand has increased for that location. You'll see this all the time in certain areas like Orlando, Florida. During spring break and just after Christmas is the busiest time in those areas, all the hotels raise their prices to crazy ridiculous numbers. At one point in time I had to raise the rate to $1,000 per night at a hotel that rarely even sold when over $100 per night.

I did that just to get people to stop booking and they were still booking at $1,000! So, I learned and made better (more profitable) plans for the next year at that time. Location is a key factor when it comes to setting your rates, make sure you take advantage of it to maximize your hotel's revenue.

Another example deals with the rate itself. If I set a rate at an economy hotel that's way too high, I'm not going to get any reservations. If I set a rate at a luxury hotel that's way too low, I'm not going to get the type of reservations that I'm looking for at that hotel. If I use the strategy where I'm giving an economy rate for a luxury property, that's an automatic loss because the type of guests that I'm going to get aren't going to make my property as appealing to the type of guest that usually stays at that luxury hotel. Your rate strategy will play a key role in your success, which is why you never base your rate decision off the lowest price alone.

And of course, we can't forget your review score. A guest would rather take a chance on an economy hotel with a great review score versus a luxury hotel with a terrible review score. Let me rephrase that: quality guests will take a chance on an economy hotel that has a great review score versus a luxury hotel that has a terrible review score. Review scores are the new gold. Your hotel is no longer qualified just by its location … the value of an asset is determined by the review score that you have in addition to the location. It is such a pivotal point when it comes to a hotel's worth you can't afford to ignore it. Make sure you're on the ball when it comes to quality. You can set all the rates correctly, but if you're not giving the service that a guest is looking for, you will rarely see them return and if it is so bad they leave a poor review – they not only won't return, but that bad review can cost you future new clients who will pass you by for another hotel.

Understanding Demand

The next thing I want to share with you is understanding demand. I have recently seen luxury hotels become quality hotels because they didn't understand demand. Just because you are in a market that has high demand doesn't mean that the market is looking for your product. There is a reason why you don't see a Ritz Carlton at truck stops. A lot of hotel owners and hotel professionals really don't understand demand in their sphere of operation and that's why they're unsuccessful when it comes to generating revenue. They build the wrong type of product that doesn't resonate with the market at that time. Or should I say they build the wrong type of product in an area that does not value it. The number one key to understanding demand is understanding where your product belongs in that market segment. Understand what role your property plays in that location in that area.

Things to do when demand is low: The first thing you should do when demand is continuously low is take a hard look at your listing. The reason why you want to take a second look at your listing is because you want to see if your presentation is still competitive with the competition in the area. Your listing must stand out, your listing has to draw attention. It may be your photos, it may be your copy (description) or it may be your price. So, look at you're listing first because 9 times out of 10, your competition is updating their listings weekly or at least monthly, and you're not seeing it because you never checked yours.

Number two, keep track of the events coming into your town. There are a lot of things going on in your town or city that you may not be seeing or paying attention to. By the time you get this information, your demand surrounding an event has increased, and you missed the boat because you're almost sold out at a much lower rate than your competition. Always keep up with what's going on in your area so you know the time periods when you need to increase your rates. A lot of events like concerts, graduations, corporate events and the like are going to increase your demand.

You want to make sure your rates reflect what is actually going on in your area and act accordingly.

And of course, number three, when demand gets low, find out where it went. There's usually a reason why the demand is low. It may be that certain events used to come to the city or town and have stopped coming, or a company left town, or several new hotels have opened and are taking your market share. The reason why you want to know why the demand is low is so that you can search out something similar. Let's say a company left town, it may be time to pursue their competition, they're not the only company in the world.

When demand is high, that's when it's time to adjust your revenue management strategy. Here are a couple of tips and tricks that work in pretty much any situation when it comes to revenue management. What happens is when demand is high? A lot of hotels remove themselves from listing platforms. The reasons why they remove themselves from OTAs (online travel agents) is because they don't want to pay the commission. The problem with this is that a lot of times when you remove yourself from the OTA, you're no longer visible to the customer. A guest can't book a hotel they can't see. You need to take advantage of this and capitalize off of it. When hotels remove themselves from the OTAs it reduces the competition on the playing field for you and gives you the advantage. When there's a high demand day, and everybody's moving their hotels from the OTAs, this is an opportunity for you to dramatically increase your rates on that platform.

The best way to do this is charge in addition to your calculation of the commission. So, if my rate is $350.49 and my commission is 15%, my OTA rate will be $403.06. This is why I have no problem paying a commission because I've calculated the fee into the transaction. I think of it as having the guest paying the commission. So why would I care about 15% when I'm not paying it anyway? When I have a low rate and I'm paying the OTA commissions, then I'm paying the commission because it's coming out my standard rate or my average rate.

When my rate is 2-3 times higher than average, that's when the guest is paying for it. When your competition blocks their inventory and takes their rooms off of the OTAs it actually works to your advantage. The second reason why it works to your advantage is people put in the wrong dates all the time. How many times have you gotten a call from a guest stating they entered the wrong dates and they need to change the date on the reservation they just booked. So if they accidentally put in a wrong date, and you removed your hotel from the OTA website, the hotel that shows up on the OTA is more than likely going to get the business. When you're removing yourself from the OTA website it means that you're not there for the guests to select. The hotel that's on the listing is going to win by default. That's why I never removed myself from the OTAs. It's just a lose/lose situation for me, for the guests, and for the OTAs.

The next revenue management tip is splitting your listings online. You may be wondering, "What's splitting my listings online?" That's when a property has multiple room types. Let's look at how it works for a suite: if a guest is looking for a suite, they're going to go to an extended stay hotel or a hotel that specializes in nothing but suites. Something like the Comfort Inn, Homewood Suites, Residence Inn or maybe a Hyatt House. Most of the time the guest doesn't even get the opportunity to see the suites in your hotel or the suite prices from your current profile. On the page on the website/listing the only thing they're seeing from you are regular hotel rooms which doesn't even give you an opportunity to compete against the hotels listed above. If guests are looking for a suite, a lot of times your property gets passed by. But if you create a second listing that displays nothing but your suites, then you'll stand out. It will give your potential client another option to see exactly what you have so that you can compete with other brands that have a similar room type.

In order to be an effective and successful revenue manager, you have to understand how a typical guest thinks. The guest doesn't look at room pickup reports. The guest doesn't look at STR reports. The guest is looking for a great hotel that matches their lifestyle. At the end of the day, it's not the revenue manager that decides what the guests pay. It's the guest's situation that decides what the guests will pay. Sometimes you'll have a luxury guest that's in a financial situation. So they have to choose a value hotel or a quality hotel. Sometimes you'll have a economy guest that has no choice but to choose a quality hotel because there's nothing else available in that area at that time. So they can either drive a million miles away from their location, or they can choose the price that is listed for the quality hotel.

Hotel Revenue Management Submarket

Another thing that you need to focus on is the submarket. Depending on where you're located, the submarket could be a couple of different things. If you're in a big city, the submarket probably will be within five miles outside of your current location. Take a map and circle five miles around your hotel. If you're out in the country, where there's very few hotels and a small population, it can be anywhere from 30 to 60 miles out! I've managed hotels that had submarkets 30 miles away. The important thing to remember is that when it comes to a submarket, travelers are also looking at that extended submarket as well.

The market any guest is searching for is going to produce the hotels around you. Whether it be through a franchise website, a search engine SEO or the like ... your hotel's submarket is going to pop up. This is the way a visitor thinks when they see the submarket. The number one thing is usually location. Now, if your submarket is only five miles away from your hotel, that means they're going to look at your rate, see the rates in that smaller geographical area. If those rates are lower in your submarket, and I mean drastically lower, they're going to think, "Well, I can drive another five miles to save $30 to $100 at this other hotel." That other hotel is out of your main market. This can bite a guest in the butt but they may not consider this. For example, an additional 5 miles in Atlanta, Georgia, could cost them another hour of driving in traffic.

The other thing you want to think about if your submarket is even farther out is: do you believe people will drive an additional 15, 20, or 30 miles just to save an additional $50? Does this change if they're staying for more than one night? To them, it's about the total they will save for their entire stay and not the total they save for a single day. They are thinking about their total vacation (or visit) budget. You have to calculate your rates not only for your market, but also for your submarket. They can't be too high so that they drive guests away into your submarket and they can't be too low so they fill up your hotel at a lower rate faster than the competition that's also in your market.

The next thing you must forecast and look out for when you're setting your rates is the vacation home rental market. Yes, you know it! People are renting vacation homes and the owners of those homes are getting their fair share of the market with Airbnb and VRBO. And now the OTAs are listing these vacation homes as well. So not only are you competing with hotels, you're also competing with anyone that wants to rent out a room in their garage or their basement! One of the things you can do to bring this into your market calculations is look at the demand. One of the easiest ways to do this is to use a website called Airdna.com which allows you to see what the rates are in the vacation home rental market. You should take a look at the rates and see how your rates compare with Airbnb. If you're in a bigger city this is going to be a little less popular versus being in a smaller town where hotels aren't as readily available and there are more Airbnb listings.

If you're looking to take your revenue management game to the next level, you can get your Revenue Management certification at the International Hospitality Institute by visiting www.internationalhospitalityinstitute.com.

The MJ of Hotels 3 Point Shot

The key to revenue management is not to let a bunch of reports dictate your decisions. A potential guest doesn't look at room pickup reports or pace reports before they make a reservation. Learn to view rates through a guest's eyes first and not what you believe a bunch reports state. Sometimes you must trust your gut and take some risks.

Hotel Sales

Group Sales
By Halee Whiting

Hotel sales is not for the weak of heart. To a hotel front desk agent it might look like a dream job full of taking clients out to lunch, bringing cookies to people ... but it is so much more. It is the sales department's role to provide a perfect sales mix for a hotel. That means making sure that your hotel is financially stable with different types of business from different market segments. A lot of hotels learned during the pandemic that it is very costly to be reliant on one type of business. We saw hotels that were dependent on just plain white-collar business travelers turn to blue collar, others that were dependent on SMERF (Social, Military, Educational, Religious and Fraternal) business come to a screaming halt.

When you diversify the sales process to include all market segments and try to evenly split them out amongst your hotel's offerings, that is when you will be most successful. The prospecting landscape has changed since the pandemic. No longer can you just drop by an office to pitch a special rate for their meetings because a lot of those offices don't exist anymore. The old saying that it takes eight or nine phone calls to close the deal is now doubled that based on businesses changing up their personnel and the harder to nail down flex-time that keeps workers on different schedules.

Prospecting Tips

Even though the sales environment has changed, the basic fundamentals of prospecting are still there. You can't assume unless you make the phone call. Now let's talk about some prospecting tips. When working in new hotels, my go to for generic corporate is to look at the top 20 employers for an area. I will also Google search different industries like auto and manufacturing to come up with lists. Another great way to find business that will immediately be reflected in your STR is by taking your competitors' phone numbers and searching them on Google. This allows you to find websites, PDFs, and other documents that your competitors are listed on and possibly not you. It is important to remember that when you're prospecting, you can't just call and say, "Hi, my name is (so and so). And I'm calling from the ABC hotel, does your company use hotels?"

You never know who's going to end up answering the phone and chances are they're probably not the decision maker and never have to deal with lodging. It's important to give more details. Here is an example, "Hi, I'm (so and so) calling from ABC hotel. Do you know who handles travel at your location? I'm looking for somebody who sets up hotel rates for employees traveling from different plants or vendors coming in to meet with you and trainings or even overnight hotel rooms for hiring people." The more details that you give somebody, the more it's going to make them think and possibly realize which department might be able to assist you. So, what happens after you've made the initial call?

You need to trace your follow up. If you can't find a good contact, try looking on LinkedIn. If you only made it to somebody's voicemail, set a trace in your calendar or CRM (Customer Relationship Management) for follow up in another week or so.

Say you're trying to court an account that is very loyal to one of your competitors. Are you touching base with them every six to eight weeks? If not, then you should be. That's a great rule of thumb for follow up. We are all human and chances are they might slip up and if you're calling consistently, you'll be the first on that contact's mind when they are unhappy with the old place.

After you've prospected, and they finally agree to stay at your hotel, it is time to negotiate your rate. What should you be thinking of? A lot of novice salespeople, especially if they're trying to steal a client from a competitor, will automatically jump to offering a very low rate. That is a huge no no and you should not be leaving money on the table. At this point in the game, you need to qualify. One of the ways that I do this is I like to ask my client what the three most important things are when it comes to selecting a hotel for them.

The answer could be price, the answer could be comps or upgrades for VIPs. It could be a shuttle; it could be a variety of things. Finding ways that you can add value to the room rate you want to give them can save you from having to lower your rate. It could be as simple as adding bonus points or a welcome snack and water bottle. Once you finally come up with what rate you would like to submit, make sure it is the highest rate you would ideally want. Remember, you generally can't negotiate up. Once you have won the business, now comes the tricky task of maintaining the relationship. This isn't just maintaining the relationship with your existing contact but finding a way to connect with guests.

This could be playing lobby lizard connecting with them at breakfast. Or if you're working remotely, 70 little gift bags and treats for guests checking in with special welcome notes. It's also important to communicate with the front desk and operation staff when you have VIP clients coming through. While you work on maintaining your relationship with a client, it is very important to make sure they're holding up their end of the bargain as well. If you're a hotel that typically sells out with a lot of corporate Tuesdays and Wednesdays, and this client is only staying on those days, there's an opportunity for growth ... it is important to check production quarterly to make sure that your client is holding up their end of the bargain.

The sales process is all about finding new business, growing it and eventually replacing it. There may be a time when you have a client that's been with you for a long time that will not budge on rate but they're staying on your high demand days; it might be time to walk away. It's important to always discuss with them first, don't kick them to the curb without giving them a reasonable explanation and an exiting time plan. When you come to the table, bring your production reports and discuss production with them; they understand the need to make a profit; don't be coy, since you are about to cut them off, you can be very honest about your need to increase rates. This conversation needs to be primarily based on facts. It can cover issues like when they originally signed this contract with your company, you were expecting that they would book 200 room nights a year and in the first quarter you've only seen 10 room nights and then only on Tuesdays and Wednesdays which are higher demand days.

You might find out that they had to downsize some things or they're going to pick up more in quarter 2 and/or quarter 3. These are all factors you should consider when it comes to renegotiating pricing as well.

Extra prospecting ideas; prospecting does not mean by phone only. Prospecting can be done in a variety of ways.

You can try outdoor drop-ins, parking lot shops, and attending community events. Parking lot shops are one of my favorite ways to convert a business helping them start faster. It's best to do parking lot shops before 7am in the morning and after seven or eight o'clock at night when all the vehicles are in the parking lot of your competitor's hotels. You can talk with your general manager or management team about incentivizing your three to eleven or night audit person to do parking lot shops when they come in or leave the hotel.

Make sure you have your phone out to take pictures, it's important to look for logos and USDOT numbers. When you attend local community events like a chamber of commerce mixer, it is important to look at these individuals in different ways. Don't just look at Mark from ABC Company as ABC Company. Mark might have family that travels to the area during the holidays.

Tips for keeping organized and productive in the sales world

Sometimes getting in prospecting calls for the week can seem very exhausting. A good rule of thumb that I usually kept when I worked on property was 10-by-10. I tried to make 10 prospecting calls by 10am in the morning. The way that I did this was at the end of my workday I would research the 10 calls that I wanted to make the next morning, set them up traced ready to go so I could just call them with no other prep work in the morning because we all know that prospecting isn't the most fun job sometimes and you have to be in the right mood to do it. Using organizational tools like a CRM to keep track of your calls will help keep you organized and know where you need to go next. If your hotel can't afford a CRM, using an Excel doc and color coding, creating different tabs for different market segments and clients can help keep you organized on a budget.

It is important to work smarter not harder. Easy new tools like AI programs and bots to prospect for you can help take some time out of your prospecting endeavors. Another great way to be productive in the sales world is to know what rates you can quote ahead of time. Sit down with your general manager and develop rate parameters for corporate accounts producing over 100 room nights a year. What rate can you offer if they commit to 200 room nights or more? It is even worth setting up a small business rate of 10 to 15% off for companies that produce under 50 room nights. Maybe they don't have enough to qualify for a full corporate account but giving them some form of a discount will keep a steady flow of incoming while making them feel appreciated; it will create loyalty to your hotel. They will stay with you and all those little guys add up.

If you're an onsite salesperson, use Monday and Fridays as your in office time and mark Tuesdays, Wednesdays and Thursdays as you're out and about days for outside calls. Having your two-admin days set up like that will allow you to set (and do any follow up) and reset for the next week. Just like we discussed earlier, it's important to check quarterly reports. Go through your company's top 50 report and challenge yourself to see if you know all the companies listed. In the same breath, it's also very important to have a great relationship with your front desk. The front desk is the unsung hero of finding sales leads. Training them on how to look for sales leads and incentivizing them when they find those leads will bring more revenue for your hotel.

In conclusion, there's three things to remember with sales: Never assume, make the calls and get creative!

Revenue Generation for Hotel Sales Teams

By Doug Kennedy

S tart by evaluating your sales incentives and bonus structure. Too many hotel sales teams are bonused only on their specific segment, thus creating an **us vs. them** mentality between transient and group, causing them to see the RM (Revenue Manager) as a barrier to meeting their sales goals. Migrate to a total revenue, RevPAR (Revenue Per Available Room) or RevPAC (Revenue Per Available Customer) model to encourage them to focus on the big picture. While you are at it, factor in a percentage of the incentive that is either added-on or subtracted, depending on how the salesperson complies with your hotels salesest habits (I like to use this term instead of best practices.)

Inbound leads are the hottest, despite the fact that we are flooded with them. Whereas in the past, buyers would reach out to hotels individually, these days at the click of a few buttons at CVENT, The Knot or a CVB (Convention and Visitors Bureau) site one buyer can send an RFP (request for proposal) to a dozen or more properties. As a result, hotel salespeople feel spammed by inbound leads, while buyers feel spammed by **generic** proposals.

Reengineer Your Sales Process

Provide your experienced sales managers with the support they need to help sort and prioritize sales inquiries. The ways this might work vary greatly according to the size and type of property you are working on. For example, those with larger sales teams should consider adding a sales coordinator. Those with smaller teams can train a front desk staffer or even a night auditor to use down-times at the desk to help out.

This person can help sift through lead channels that are notoriously filled with random, weak lead channels. (I won't risk offending these providers by naming them here, but everyone in hotel sales knows which ones I am talking about!) The staff can look through the long list of weak leads that simply say "send me your wedding planner" or "I need a block of rooms. What are the rates?" or that say they are looking for dates that are already sold out, or who state they are looking for rates considerably lower than your ranges.

Your coordinator can identify and forward the truly right sized, hot leads on to a salesperson. They can then continue to at least reply to other weak leads in a personalized way so as to clarify vague requests, to notify them that requested dates are sold-out and see if they might become flexible or let them know that rates requested are not in your range. Whereas at most hotels these weak leads are not even responded to, having a back-up person at least respond will definitely sift out the sand and leave some decent nuggets in the pan, perhaps gaining you a new client.

Conduct A Sales Process Assessment

Sit with each salesperson and ask them to explain their process for fielding a right sized lead that is for open dates, which of course should be in compliance with your hotel's stated best habits. Then ask them to show you where they store leads from the past, usually an Outlook folder or even an old-school stack of printed copies of RFPs in a file folder.

Then randomly select a handful of these old leads and ask the salesperson to document how and when they followed-up. Was the sales collateral (such as a PDF or electronic proposal) sent personalized? Were they tenacious and timely in following up? Were the follow-up messages also personalized? Did they use a mix of follow-up mediums such as calls and emails? If a lead for a recurring event or meeting was lost, did they trace it for follow-up next year?

This sales assessment exercise is something we have frequently done for our KTN hotel sales training clients and the results can be shocking for some leaders. Our experience shows that about 20% of hotel salespeople are completely on top of managing their sales process, while another 20% are basically glorified order-takers. Most salespeople are somewhere in between, and they can be challenged to perform to a higher level, especially when told this exercise will be repeated in a few months (stick) while encouraging them close more to up their commission (carrot).

Collaborate With the Director of Sales on Standards (a.k.a. Best Habits)

If you have not already done so, after performing the aforementioned assessment, it is a good idea to then set standardized expectations for how future sales leads are to be processed from start to finish. While a timely response is key, the theory that the person who responds first is most likely to get the deal is an urban legend. In fact, many buyers complain that respondents miss key details from the inquiry or RFP.

Instead, balance a fast response time with a proposal that is personalized and contextualized. What is your standard for personalization? If sent by email, do we ask the recipient to confirm receipt? Do we follow-up 3-5 business days later? Do we vary the follow-up messaging so as not to send three guilt-inducing emails or to leave three voicemails complaining that we've not heard back from them yet? If lost, do we retrace? If won, after the booking is fulfilled, do we follow-up to ask for referrals?

Train Yourself, Then Your Team To Embrace Their CRM

Again, our experience working with hotel sales training clients of all segments shows that most hotel salespeople are not maximizing their use of whatever sales CRM they have in place. In all fairness, this is usually no fault of their own. For one, the sales CRM their executive leaders have selected might be confusing and overwhelming to use, having been purchased by an IT-minded person who was overly impressed with a proliferation of features that are not needed and rarely used.

Also, the CRM may have been improperly set-up by a systems administrator. One such example: When a piece of business turns definite, many CRMs then generate numerous auto-tasks that populate the sales task list causing an overwhelming number of tasks to appear daily. Because most RGMs tend to be tech-savvy and to be masters of process, they are likely to have the unique skill sets needed to help reengineer the sales CRM to better meet the needs of the sales team.

Ensure Your Team Is Prospecting Proactively

If all your salespeople do is to close incoming leads, they are practicing sales fishing. They hold their "fishing pole" that is connected to a line holding a hook. On the hook is the digital bait, which is your website presence, listing on CVENT or Wedding Wire, and/or the brand.com flag. Once a prospect "bites," they reel-in the business. A true hotel sales professional embraces sales hunting. They go out and hunt down new business that is not otherwise coming in.

Unfortunately, proactive prospecting is rarely practiced in today's hotel sales departments. Our experience in conducting sales process assessments shows that when prospecting **is** happening, it's usually not done well. For example, when a Director of Sales or General Manager mandates X number of prospecting attempts per month, a salesperson will simply send X number of generic emails or send X number of LinkedIn messages or make X number of phone calls. Again, being the masters of process, RGMs can greatly assist in mentoring and training hotel salespeople for proactive prospecting.

Research Before You Reach Out

As a member of the LinkedIn community myself, at least a few times a month I get random messages from hoteliers who somehow think I am either a meeting planner or a corporate travel manager. Their messages are some version of this: "Hi. I am the sales manager for Brand X Hotel in Anytown. We are a newly renovated 200 room hotel that features a sparking pool, a hearty breakfast with fresh hot waffles and complimentary Wi-Fi. Let me know if you would like to book with us." These messages waste time and turn off real prospects and some are so far from my location that they are laughable.

Alternatively, with so much information online, it is easier than ever to quickly research and then personalize prospecting messaging. Here's an example of one I would definitely respond to: "Hello Douglas. Thanks for accepting my connection request. I noticed that KTN holds two-day sales training events in several cities each year. Although I didn't see that you have yet been to Anytown, I was wondering if you might consider holding one of your events here. If so, I would love to have a chance to connect so I could discover a bit more about your needs and then if it makes sense to send over a detailed proposal."

Train Your Team to Use A Tech For Touch

Approach. Again, RGMs are usually uniquely skilled at both people and process, and can help your sales teams use some of the same tools you use to manage revenue. One example is Calendly which is a free scheduling app that makes it easy for a lead you are prospecting to book onto your Outlook or Gmail schedule for a call vs. just emailing back and forth. A second example is to conduct sales calls by way of Zoom versus phone only or just an email exchange. A third example is to use personalized video email messages to put faces with names, such as sending a note to a prospect while standing in the lobby, or in a meeting/event venue, or in front of a TV on which you project a slide with their name and logo. Vidyard is an example of such a video email app that offers a free basic service.

Turn Front Desk Staff into Prospecting Partners

Perhaps the best place to look for prospective business is among hotel guests you currently have in-house. The front desk staff is uniquely positioned to assist you with identifying potential repeat guests, especially those representing companies that are booking multiple guests every time. Also, many SMERF prospects, especially those looking for wedding blocks, amateur sports team coaches, high school volunteers (parents who head-up volunteer groups for student groups in band, debate and sports), and those who have blue collar travelers may call directly or even walk-in in person to ask about special rates. Our research shows that all too often they are told to call back during business hours or blindly transferred to a voicemail. Instead, train your team to see themselves as being an extension of the sales department. Recognize, celebrate and reward them for obtaining leads to pass along to sales.

Prospect Previous Contacts

Just about every piece of business serviced by a hotel can be a source to prospect for new business. Obviously, if a meeting or event is recurring, the lead should be retraced for the next cycle. If a deal was lost, retrace for next year. Contact those who have planned corporate meetings or events to say, "I'm reaching out to say I would be very grateful if you could refer me to others at Acme Company who might be planning additional events." SMERF business leads such as sports teams or other groups of travelers might be a source of referrals from other coaches or parent volunteers from other activities. In other words, the parent volunteer who planned the team's travel to their debate contest might have a kid in the marching band and know the Band Parent Association president. The coach of the women's softball team might know the coach for soccer.

As we look toward the future of the profession, those who hold a narrow view of themselves as revenue managers may find that their roles are replaced by increasingly smart artificial intelligence and automation in general. However, those who hold an expanded view of their role will always have significant career opportunities.

Maximizing Catering and Meeting Room Sales

By Deborah Gardner, CMP, CVP

In the bustling world of hospitality, where every interaction counts and every booking matters, the journey to success often hinges on a simple yet profound principle that helps maximize catering and meeting room sales.

As a 30⁺ seasoned sales and catering professional, I have navigated many different landscapes in the world of hospitality. Today, training many industry organizations, I've found that despite facing numerous challenges – from fluctuating market demands to unexpected setbacks – I consistently noticed those that emerge successfully thanks to a steadfast commitment to what I call the power of CARE habits. Let's explore what this stands for and how I've been able to help transform the world of sales and catering.

Communication: Establishing effective communication from the outset is paramount. Whether engaging with clients or collaborating with team members, it lays the groundwork for trust, which is the cornerstone of exceptional service.

One example - amid the chaos and uncertainty of 9/11, Delta Airlines emerged as a beacon of resilience and compassion. As one of the industry's leading airlines, their response to the crisis was nothing short of remarkable, demonstrating the power of effective communication in the face of adversity.

In an era where there were no cell phones and social media, communication was challenging, Delta Airlines (back then called Continental Airlines) had a special telephone number for their employees to call anytime to receive company updates, ask questions, and receive other useful matters. It was a successful strategy that helped close the gap between employees and the leadership team. Where this simple strategy paid off was when 9/11 happened, all the employees knew to pick up the telephone, whether a phone booth or office phone. Delta had all the instructions on what everyone needed to do immediately. This type of prepared model allowed Delta Airlines to rise to the occasion with their customers too. They personally reached out to each of their customers to provide clarity and reassurance. They didn't just inform; they empathized, ensuring passengers understood what had happened and how Delta would support them by easing their concerns like re-booking their flights.

Delta's exemplary response serves as a timeless reminder that effective communication is not just about conveying information—it's about instilling trust, building relationships, and providing support when it matters most.

This proactive approach left an indelible mark on their customers, highlighting the importance of clear communication in times of crisis. By following in Delta's footsteps, sales and catering professionals can navigate challenges with confidence, knowing that clear and compassionate communication will always leave a lasting impression on their customers, especially in times of crisis. How many times do we deal with a crisis, right? This commitment to communication fosters trust and transparency, laying the foundation for successful partnerships for many years to come.

Acquisition - Securing a consistent flow of business is paramount for success. Obtaining or acquiring something important can be done through an acquisition process. In the context of business and sales, acquisition often refers to acquiring a stream of income of leads with customers or prospects which is essential for generating revenue and growing a business. To identify and nurture leads effectively use diverse methods—advertising, social media engagement, direct marketing, and referrals.

However, the most forgotten yet most powerful source of leads lies within your existing customer base. Transforming customers into fans generates organic brand advocacy. Cultivate genuine relationships and personalized interactions then empower them to become ambassadors for your brand. Embrace this shift and witness the transformative power of fan-driven growth. It's not merely about transactions; it's about forging lasting connections and partnerships. Sometimes, these interactions evolve into friendships, rooted in a deep understanding of each other's needs and values. While it demands dedication and time, the outcomes are invaluable. Maintaining consistent communication is essential; don't just move on after a sale, but foster a lasting bond.

Think of your business not as a one-time destination but a continuous journey where customers are not just shoppers but loyal advocates. Utilize CRM systems to personalize interactions, keeping track of their milestones and interests. By prioritizing this relationship-building approach, you ensure a steady stream of leads. Always ask for repeat business and referrals so your fans feel valued and empowered. It's not merely about transactions; it's about cultivating a culture of loyalty and trust that propels your business forward.

For example, having a social media strategy is very powerful.

It's an effective way to disseminate ideas and keep your audience engaged. Sharing tips related to your products or services not only educates your audience but also subtly promotes your offerings. By providing valuable information, you position yourself as an authority in your field, staying top-of-mind for potential customers.

For instance, my Hospitality Home Watch and Services business caters to snowbirds in Arizona. Utilizing social media, I share home maintenance tips to my predominantly Canadian, Californian, Wisconsinite and Minnesotan clientele. Whether it's fixing leaky faucets or preparing homes for seasonal changes, these tips resonate with them, reinforcing my expertise, fostering trust which turns into business. The result? We have been servicing the same fifty (and growing) customers consistently for 5 years now.

Staying connected with your customers or guests through regular, informative content not only strengthens existing relationships but also cultivates new leads. By leveraging your customer base as advocates, you create a cycle of loyalty and referral that drives sustained business growth. Utilize social media as a powerful tool to educate, engage, and ultimately, convert leads into loyal fans.

Ratio - Despite receiving last-minute leads or serving repeat clients, there's always room for upgraded services through value-based selling. Yet, this type of closing ratio is often overlooked by catering departments. It is a crucial step for maximizing profits and satisfying customers.

Here's the key: when you prioritize value-based selling, both your bottom line and customer satisfaction levels skyrocket. Surveys reveal that 92% of buyers crave a value proposition early in conversations, feeling valued and attended to. So, take advantage of every proposal or lead as an opportunity to showcase your value proposition, addressing their specific concerns and making them feel special.

Encourage your team to cultivate deeper relationships with prospects, understanding their needs and offering tailored solutions. Embracing value-based selling yields numerous benefits, including increased customer loyalty, higher conversion rates, and enhanced brand reputation. By prioritizing value, you not only elevate your closing ratio strategy but also foster long-term customer loyalty and business growth. How?

First and foremost, alleviate your prospect's anxieties by highlighting the benefits upfront. Avoid discussing price prematurely, even if they bring it up. Instead, focus on showcasing the value you offer before diving into the cost. It's a common scenario, especially in the wedding and conference venue industry, where clients are eager to know the price. However, remember this golden rule: whoever mentions price first loses. So, resist the urge to divulge it and concentrate on understanding their investment goals. Use the term "investment" rather than "budget" to convey a positive tone and emphasize the value they'll receive.

Next, educate your clients by offering something unique and unprecedented. What sets your hotel and/or services apart? Highlighting these distinctive features is the essence of value-based selling. Encourage creativity within your team to identify novel selling points that resonate with clients and ultimately boost revenue.

Lastly, understanding your competition is fundamental. Differentiate your offerings by innovating where others don't. Present your value additions effectively, whether it's during meetings or on site inspections. Involving leadership in value-based selling amplifies the team effort, enhancing client engagement and satisfaction. Collaborate with key stakeholders, like the general manager, to help reinforce your sales pitch and demonstrate a team effort.

In essence, thorough preparation and strategic collaboration, you pave the way for successful value-based selling. By prioritizing value over price, educating clients, and leveraging team synergy, you can elevate your sales approach and drive impressive closing ratio results.

Expectations: Throughout our life, we have expectations of our selves, of others. They are our beliefs. They can be based on past experiences, societal norms, or personal desires, and they often influence our thoughts, emotions, and behaviors. To make sure our outcomes match the expectations we want, you have to have patience.

Advocating for your product's value requires time, especially with potential customers. Rushing to sell the perfect package on the first encounter can backfire. Buyers are cautious; they perceive sales and catering professionals as uniform and insincere. However, to set yourself apart, it's about providing genuine value.

In other words, it all starts with you—the value-based seller. Your rapport and authenticity are paramount, fostering lasting connections and financial success. With each interaction, you're not just selling; you're building trust and propelling your organization to new heights.

The renowned sales expert, Brian Tracy, believes in staying in the moment by using a technique that transcends hesitation called The Invitational Close. When prospects show interest but hesitate, remove the commitment. Say, "Let's continue this tomorrow" or "Take a look at these options." This simple act empowers them, easing budget concerns and prompting action. Here are a few more ideas …

Prepare. Have everything ready: the contract, the details—all tailored to their needs. Invite them to commit. Tracy emphasizes this as a pivotal moment—a private alliance between seller and prospect. Seize it, and revenues soar.

Invite, don't persuade. "If you like it, take it," or "Let's consider this." Maintain the dialogue. When doubts wane and silence speaks volumes, they often accept. Don't ever let them leave empty-handed.

React strategically. If met with reluctance, one of my all time favorite technique is to *flinch*. Yep! It's a fun attention getter when you show your emotional side - pleased or disappointed. Let them gauge your conviction, knowing you won't easily concede to their decision.

For example, imagine you're at a car dealership, eyeing that sleek new model. The salesperson lays out all the features, offering you a test drive. You're impressed but hesitant. You mentioned you might think about it and come back later. This is the pivotal moment—the salesperson's chance to close the deal. Just like on the car lot, if you leave without making a decision, chances are slim you'll return. The salesperson understands the importance of seizing the moment. They maintain their composure but subtly flinch when you hesitate. It's not about pressuring you; it's about showing their commitment and confidence in the product. You sense their conviction and realize this isn't just another sales pitch—it's an opportunity. Feeling reassured, you decide to take the plunge and drive off in that new car today.

In the world of sales, timing is everything. Tracy's Invitational Close is a masterstroke, bridging hesitancy with opportunity. Be ready, be assertive, and watch as prospects transform into clients. And a simple flinch can make all the difference between a missed opportunity and a successful sale. It's about keeping the conversation flowing and nudging them towards a decision.

But there's more to improving your sales process. Shift your mindset from selling to persuasion. Instead of waiting for customers to come to you, you must proactively pull them in. Ever thought about creating and personalizing an e-newsletters from the catering department? It's a powerful technique. Whether it's a class reunion or a wedding, these newsletters keep you top of mind and help boost sales for the entire hotel.

But mindset alone isn't enough; you need tactics to guide your journey. Enter the idea of a vision board. It may seem gimmicky, but it's a potent tool for visualizing your future success. By assembling images and phrases that reflect everyone's ambitions, you create a tangible reminder of why you're striving for the goal. Sharing a vision board with others adds another dimension—it sparks conversations and showcases your aspirations for the entire team and hotel.

Remember, success in catering (or any field) is measured by your activity and results above expectations. It's a tough benchmark to meet, but with the right mindset and tools like the e-newsletter and vision board ideas, you're well-equipped to navigate the challenges and achieve revenue goals.

Overall, consistency is the cornerstone of success, especially in sales. While anyone can be a good sales representative, it takes a high performer to consistently exceed their goals. The four CARE habits—effective communication, acquisition maintaining a regular stream of leads through acquisitions, improving closing ratio, and embracing value-based selling expectations proves that process works.

As a leader, incorporating the CARE habits into your daily routine isn't just about checking off boxes; it's about genuinely caring about your customers and their needs. By consistently applying these principles, you'll not only close more deals but also foster stronger relationships and drive greater revenue than ever before.

So let's commit to CARE—to caring deeply about our customers, our team, and our goals. Together, we can create an environment where success is not just a possibility but an inevitability. Let's CARE our way to unparalleled success!

Front Desk Sales & Revenue Management

By Doug Kennedy
Revenue Managers Should Transition
To Revenue Generators

Managing Front Office & Hotel Sales Teams

I f you ask most hoteliers to write up a job description for the position of Revenue Manager (RM), chances are the responsibilities listed would focus on controlling and "managing" revenue channels. For example, the first thing that comes to mind might be setting rates and restrictions for transient segments, determining channel mix based on net revenues, calculating revenue-per-guest opportunities, and providing sales staff with quotes for groups and functions.

However, all too often the biggest opportunity is overlooked, which is for RMs to increase RevPAR and RevPAC to generate revenue by being the champion of hotel sales excellence. Perhaps it is time for the lodging industry to reimagine this title from Revenue Manager (which implies a passive role in managing revenue that is generated elsewhere) to a more active label: Revenue Generator Manager (RGM). Because of the position which RMs hold on most org-charts, either overseeing or having a dotted line to the sales and front office silos, they are uniquely positioned to help leaders of both departments recognize and actualize revenue generating opportunities.

Of course, the role of RMs, as well as the revenue generating opportunities, varies greatly by property according to factors such as:

- Size of lodging operations and segment of lodging. Obviously, properties that have fewer rooms and lower rates will have fewer leadership roles, so the standard RM's job would likely include operational, sales and marketing responsibilities, whereas at larger properties they would have a specialized focus.

- Variance of room types. Properties having one to a few room categories with few points of differentiation will have fewer opportunities to upsell by accommodation type. However, smart RMs can still develop clever rate options. However, where there are more categories and classifications of rooms, there are more levers to pull for a RM.

- Number of revenue-generating outlets. The more outlets, the greater the number of opportunities to generate more revenue-per-guest from Food and Beverage spa, recreational activities, retail and in-house events.

- Location, and thus, market segment opportunities. RMs at properties in destinations that appeal to multiple segments can leverage corporate group, leisure group, BT, transient business and transient social segments, whereas RMs at properties that serve primarily only one segment will have fewer opportunities.

Therefore, depending on the above factors, a Revenue Manager can use some – and at some hotels perhaps all – of the following ideas to migrate towards a new role as Revenue Generation Manager (RGM).

Revenue Generation for Transient Segments

Focus On Voice. Too many RMs buy into the fallacies that voice is a dying distribution channel, that only older guests who are not tech savvy call anymore, and that Millennials and Gen-Z travelers who grew up with smartphones hate actually having to talk to a customer service rep. Smart RGMs recognize that the decision to call vs. book online is situationally driven. In other words, the higher the rate, the longer the stay, the more complicated the travel plans, and in essence, the more emotionally connected they are to their travel plans … the more likely they are to call. That being said, when you talk with the front desk staff even at branded, moderate and economy lodging properties, they will tell you they still frequently receive direct inquiry calls that start with some version of: "Hi, are you actually at the hotel? Oh good. I'm thinking of staying there and I have a question…" Similarly, there often is an interplay of voice and online channels. In other words, a significant number of guests call prior to booking online, while others book online and then call.

Action steps:

- Post your phone number prominently on both desktop and mobile website versions.
- If you have on-site reservations, indicate such by adding copy that reads "Call us directly now" or "Call our local area experts."
- Provide a small incentive to staff, such as "a buck for a booking," ideally paid in cash, to encourage front desk and reservations

staff to see themselves as order-makers vs. order-takers. Even if you are more generous and offer a few bucks, it will still be far less than would be paid to a third-party platform that charges commissions.

- Use a phone provider that provides unique numbers and call tracking to determine how many calls are being generated by various digital sources such as email blasts, social media campaigns, and website paid and organic searches. Staff accordingly.

- Use a system to tag calls with a disposition or resolution code, according to whether it is a sales opportunity or service call. Some phone providers offer call tagging by pressing a number at the end; some PMS systems allow staff to take date/rate searches. This allows you to not only measure net call conversion, but also to track by denial codes for use in future rate forecasting.

- Your tag system should define any call from someone who is calling for rates or who has a specific question, such as about parking, amenities or services, as an inquiry. Everything else is a service call or general question. (This is because no one calls just to check a rate or to find out how much parking is unless they are considering a stay.)

- Retarget voice leads. Of course, you want to train your team to offer to secure the sale, and if resisted, to create urgency (availability is limited… the rate could change…) and to remove barriers (you can always cancel until…). However, some callers are simply not ready to book for whatever reason. Perhaps they need to book flights or share the details with traveling companions. Staff should then say, "Okay, well then let me grab your email address so I can shoot you over an email with my direct contact information. What's your email?"

All it takes from there is about one minute for them to pull down a template, drop-in a personalized introductory sentence or two, and then click send to capitalize on the connection. If you really want to do it right, have your staff track these leads even if just on an Excel form and then to either send a follow-up email or make a quick call a few days later to say, "I'm just checking to see what else we can do on our end to win the opportunity to host your visit."

- Consider the revenue per call opportunity. Need help convincing your operational associates of how important all this is? Calculate the opportunity that each ringing phone line creates. Take your total transient revenue divided by the number of transient stays.
- OTA (Online Travel Agent) Questions Are Leads. Most hotels experience a significant attrition or "wash" of OTA bookings. To encourage guests who book online to keep and not cancel, train your team to personalize their responses to questions that come through OTAs after booking but prior to arrival.
- Start by taking a look at the reply to messages currently being sent by your team. For example, if a sender says, "Can we park a motorcycle trailer (or RV)?" chances are your team's standard reply is a yes. Instead, they should be recognizing this as a chance to make a personal connection such as this: "Hello *Douglas!* I'm Chris at the front desk (or reservations). It is wonderful to hear from you and absolutely yes! We can definitely accommodate your motorcycle trailer during your stay. If you have any other questions or requests, just reply or call us directly here on-site. We look forward to hosting you."

Now, this might seem like a lot of typing, but in fact it can all be copied/pasted, as the only part that is personalized is in *italics*.

Focus on walk-in opportunities. Especially at hotels located along highway corridors, capturing walk-ins still reflects a revenue opportunity. Train staff on how to respond to the standard question of "Hi, do you have rooms tonight? What's the rate?" by engaging the traveler in a conversation as they search for rates. Train them to offer specific details about the room type available such as "I have a quiet 2nd floor room at the end of the hallway near the stairwell, or if you have a lot of luggage, I can get you right next to the elevator." Train them to offer two room categories, not just the lowest priced one.

Channel conversion. Of course, any RM knows that direct booking channels are the most profitable because the property saves on commissions and owns the guest contact record for future promotions. However, the battle for direct bookings is like hand-to-hand combat won by making stronger, personal connections with all guests.

- Add copy to your website that reads: Call directly for the lowest rates and phone-only specials.
- As most OTAs only restrict hotels from underselling them by way of digital channels, a workable solution is to offer slightly lower phone only rates, or an upgrade, or a guaranteed room type/location, or an extra amenity.
- Train front desk staff to obtain email addresses at registration by saying why they want an email, such as "To send you a receipt for any incidental charges" or "to notify you in the event of any lost and found items."
- At hotels catering to frequent business travelers, encourage front desk staff to offer to rebook guests at departure. "Douglas, since I have all of your info right here, can I rebook your next visit and block a specific room for you?"

The MJ of Hotels 3 Point Shot

The number one thing a sales team needs is leads. Some people hustle for them with parking lot shops, Google searches, and networking. Others just sit by the phone and take orders or try to get them from a guest that's already in-house. There is a way to get qualified leads by putting your tax dollars to work. Why go through all that work when you can just get your first set of leads from the government? Every state has their own version of the Federal Freedom of Information Act. In most states it is called the Open Public Records Request Act.

You can request the business name, address, phone number, email address, and the amount of money the state, city, or county the government spent with their vendor. The type of vendors the government pays can range from highway construction, to out of state contractors, to other federal and state representatives visiting from out of town. You can even request a detailed trial balance report by date to see how often they come to your area to do business. Imagine knowing exactly how much money your prospect made before you even pick up the phone and you know when they are most likely coming back. That is the power of being in the know; to take the short road, versus not knowing and taking the long road. This works great for getting business transient guests and construction guest leads. Work smarter, not harder. Every state is different so read the laws for your state before you submit a public record request.

Increasing Revenue at the Front Desk

By Bruce Jordan

**All revenue is made or lost at the front desk
– Bruce Jordan MJ of Hotels (author)**

The front desk is the first line of defense when it comes to making, retaining, and losing revenue. I've seen guests walk out the door because they didn't like the way a front desk agent made a statement. I've seen whole groups cancel because the information about the group wasn't delivered to the front desk in a timely manner so they could disseminate the information properly to service that group.

First, let's start off with why your hotel doesn't sell more upgrades. In my hotel review show Hotel Management Do's and Don'ts. The biggest mistake I see is that your hotel sales process for the upgrade *begins* at the front desk instead of *ending* at the front desk. Yes, it begins at the front desk instead of ending at the front desk.

There is no reason why your hotel's upgrade process should begin at the front desk. Let me give you an example. If we all know an upgrade is the bread and butter of hotel front desk sells, then it should be everywhere. You should be talking about upgrades in your listing, you should be talking about upgrades on your telephone's hold music. You should be talking about upgrades in emails and confirmation emails, you should be talking about upgrades on phone calls and reservation calls, everybody should be talking about possible upgrades. It should **not** begin at the front desk.

You should be talking about the upgrade options so much, by the time a guest gets to the front desk and the front desk agent asks them about an upgrade, the guest is so curious the next question that comes out of their mouth is, "What's included in the upgrade?" This is the response you are looking for when front desk staff presents an upgrade offer to a guest. But this is what usually happens: when guests get to the front desk as soon as staff presents the upgrade offer to the customer the answer is already "no" because it's the first-time the guest is hearing about an upgrade and to them upgrade just means more money. They don't want to spend more money, so they don't want an upgrade. No upgrade sells mean zero additional revenue. All because you're not incorporating the sale of the upgrade into your entire communication process.

How many hotels want to sell more upgrades? Now the next big mistake that I see is the pricing of those upgrades. I see hotels that have the same room as the regular room that they're trying to sell as an upgraded one: same size, same everything. They have this hotel room at $100 or more per night, that doesn't make any sense. Most hotels are pricing themselves out of the market, the price is so high the front desk agent can't sell the upgrade.

The next problem I see a lot is there aren't enough upgrade rooms to sell. Most hotels confuse upgrades with suites, and this couldn't be further from the truth. An upgraded room is a room that has a unique feature that other rooms don't have. It can be a view (sunset view, pool view, etc), it can be a location (1st floor close to an exit), and/or a feature that no other room has (premium bedding, massaging shower, 75-inch smart TV, etc.). To get more info on how to turn regular rooms into upgrades please visit hotelrevenuebible.com/upgrade.

10 to 20 percent of your hotel's inventory should be comprised of upgrade rooms. Your upgraded rooms should never be reduced to just one or two rooms. By limiting the number of available upgraded rooms you're not only limiting the amount of revenue the front desk can generate, but you're also taking away a key tool the front desk uses to handle issues that sometimes arise with guest. If your hotel needs a guest to sign up for your franchise rewards program, offer them a free upgrade to sign up. If a VIP rewards member comes to check in, offer them a free upgrade to a pool view room instead of giving them points. If a guest has a maintenance issue and needs a room move, offer them a free upgrade to a room that has premium bedding.

Unless it's a suite or premium upgrade, I don't recommend issuing per night upgrade fees for these types of rooms. I would rather just do one lump sum amount or a onetime upgrade fee. This way, if I need to drop the upgrade fee or raise the upgrade fee it is done in an instant, the fee goes across the board. My lower level upgrade rooms are the rooms that I want to get out of the way first. I want to sell them first because I know that I'm going to get more money for these rooms than I would for a standard room. Once I'm out of lower level upgrade rooms, then I can focus on the rest of the rooms on my list. The reason why you want different levels of upgrade rooms is so you aren't pricing yourself out of the market when it comes to upgrades.

The third problem that you run into when selling a hotel upgrade when it comes to rooms is the front desk when front staff doesn't want to sell these upgrades. I had the same problems when I was selling upgrades, they were complaining, saying it can't be done. They claimed that nobody wanted to buy these upgraded rooms for the extra fee, and so on and so forth. What I did was I worked at the front desk side by side with the doubtful staff. I sold five upgrades in one day right in front of their face. I made an additional $500 for the hotel. No one can tell a manager it can't be done once they are schooled that way. Actually, after the first two sold, they started looking at me and taking notes. Always give the front desk commissions on upgrades they sell. The commission could be anywhere from 20% to 50%.

A lot of people think that talking about a room upgrade so often is a little too extreme. There was this movie with this famous actor named Will Smith (I hope I don't get slapped for this): the movie was called *Focus*. In this movie he made a bet with another gentleman in a booth at a football game. He said, "I want you to pick the number of a player that's on the football field." He bet a million dollars that he could pick the exact number. The guy other guy jumped on the opportunity. The guy was looking in the stands and looking at the field. Finally, he picked the number and asks Nicky (Will Smith's character) what it was. Nicky replied that the number was 33.

The guy was surprised, he didn't know how Will Smith's character could have picked that number. What he didn't know was that Nicky had been subliminally giving him the number 33 throughout the whole day. Here is how you can capitalize on this concept: your subliminal message inside of hold music states upgrades are available several times. There are upgrade buttons on your website. When selling upgrades to guests, lead them to pick the upgrade, or at least inquire about the upgrade because if they don't do that, it significantly reduces your chance to close the deal. Be creative about where and how you pepper the environment to put upgrades at the top of an incoming guest's mind.

Now, when talking about upgrades, we're talking about hundreds of thousands of dollars in revenue that you can capture or lose. So please keep this in mind. Worst case scenario, you can give away an upgrade if the guests have an issue or bad experience. You don't have to give them a full refund. If they paid for an upgrade before their issue you can just refund the upgrade. If you don't charge for an upgrade, you must refund the actual revenue generated by the reservation, no one wants to do that. For those of you that think you still can't sell upgrades, I have an upgrade challenge. This is how it's going to work: I'm going to sell your upgrades for you. For one day, whatever I sell, you keep 100% of the money.

You have nothing to lose ... I sell it, you keep the money for one day. I do all the work, you keep all the money. Go to hotelrevenueblble. com/upgrades to learn more. Please don't pick a slow day, give me some wiggle room, give me a date that you have a good amount of check-ins. I can make it fast, easy, and simple. Also, please have a room reserved for me to use as my upgrade. I don't want the upgrade room to be a regular room, there has to be something inside the room that is special, give me something to sell. Once I am finished, you'll see how easy it is for you to sell upgrades. Let the upgrade selling begin.

Hotel Marketing Intro

This section of the book is probably the longest section for obvious reasons, it covers why OTAs exists and the reason why we're getting beat left and right as the OTAs are out marketing us. Expedia spent $7 billion on marketing, then they made 8 billion in revenue! So that lets you know how much Expedia believes in marketing. OTAs don't own the products they sell but are able to generate 8 billion dollars in revenue. All they have is a website that everyone knows about. The reason most guests are choosing OTA websites over your website is because you don't market your hotel effectively.

Most hotels are not using enough financial resources to get their property known. In addition, they are not using enough content to get their property through times when demand is low. Most hotels don't know enough about marketing to even see the value it can bring. So, when you don't value marketing at all and instead choose to pay 15%, 20% and in some cases 25% of your revenue for a reservation that you could have gotten for a couple of dollars ... it is because you don't have the tools you need to market effectively.

In this chapter, we're going to provide you with the tools you need to get started. Anyone can start getting more direct bookings, but what most hotels need is a system to covert OTA guests into permanent, loyal customers. This chapter will cover some of the marketing tools available for you to start highlighting your hotel to get more direct bookings and to pay less in commissions.

Digital Marketing

By Craig Carbonniere

Optimizing for the Future

Content visibility for hotels to capture the new wave of travel.

The world is well into taking cautious steps out from under the burden of pandemic restrictions. People are primed to travel again. They are ready to start exploring, and your business is prepared to grow.

Travelers are here; it is time for your hotel to respond.

Interestingly, many of these travelers have also demonstrated an interest in booking directly with hotels. Kalibri Labs found that direct bookings had increased by 18.2% year over year (YoY) in February 2021. These direct bookings are also more profitable than those made through third parties, making them highly desirable for your hotel.

Fortunately, as these travelers prepare to start booking their latest destinations and finding new places to explore, you and your hotel can be positioned to seize traffic and build your brand. Your website and your digital presence are about to become front and center.

As these travelers prepare for their new adventures, they turn to search and online resources with incredible regularity: 86% of travelers report using online resources when deciding on accommodations, and 73% say they use them when deciding on a destination. Additionally, 74% of travelers say they use search engines as a resource when looking for information and inspiration for their next trip.

This presents hotels with an opportunity to shine. Well-optimized content and creative digital marketing campaigns can attract these users and bring in travelers. However, many hotels struggle with content visibility. Customers might search online for information, but they don't discover the material that the hotels have posted. Hotels have to compete against online travel agents and other hotels in their area as well as price point, making competition fierce and the penalty for remaining invisible steep.

However, there is a formula that hotels can use to position their hotels to shine and take advantage of new opportunities that the future brings.

I have identified five critical steps hotels can take to boost their content visibility and get their brand in front of interested travelers. Let's explore each to see how they will increase hotel traffic and direct bookings.

Five ways hotels can increase revenue with digital marketing.

1. Getting started with website optimization

The heart of digital marketing lies on your website. Your home page on the web will provide users with a better understanding of your brand and what you offer travelers. However, this website must be designed for modern digital users. This means your site has to be developed for speed and mobile (phone) users.

The need for (website) speed

First, consider how people get to your site. Organic search accounts for 44 percent of the traffic that lands on hotel websites, which means that people come in from the search engines and click on your hotel in the Search Engine Results Page (SERP). Google is the overwhelming favorite for these users conducting searches, representing 91 percent of hotel website searches.

To make yourself appealing to these searchers and boost your rankings on Google results, you need to pay close attention to your page loading speed and your core web vitals. Google has announced explicitly that its algorithm takes loading speed into account when ranking websites.

You can go to PageSpeed Insights to get a readout of how your website performs on both desktop and mobile versions. If your website does not perform well, this is one of the first areas you will want to fix. You can also get concrete ideas about boosting your page speed directly from your results. Google will tell you if you have excessive DOM size or unused Javascript that could slow your site, for example.

Areas to watch for that can impact your site speed include:

- Image sizes
- The number of HTTP requests your site makes
- How many external scripts your site relies on
- Whether or not you have taken advantage of caching

Once you have optimized for these page speed issues, you need to set up your site for mobile users.

Optimizing for mobile users

Among travelers, mobile devices have continued to explode in usage. In 2020, amid the pandemic, the revenue generated from mobile devices increased by 26 percent. This has only continued to grow.

To capture the attention of these on-the-go users, you have two main tools at your fingertips.

Tool 1. Accelerate Mobile Pages (AMP). AMP has been around for a while, but many hotels have not taken advantage of its potential. Milestone conducted research and found that converting pages to AMP for a hotel resulted in an 83 percent increase in mobile transactions and a 68 percent increase in conversion rates.

You can use AMP to enhance customer access to critical website pages, such as the latest news, information about local attractions, and content that establishes you as one of the leading hotels in your region. Creating a positive user experience and helping them gather information about your destination will build your reputation and your chance to entice site browsers and leads.

Tool 2. Progressive web apps (PWA). With a progressive web app, your customers can access all the benefits of interacting with your brand through an app without leaving the browser window. They don't have to download anything to engage with your business. Additionally, they can use the PWA without connectivity, which creates an even more convenient experience for the users.

Trivago, for example, has emerged as a world-leading hotel search engine with its PWA. Using this web app increased user engagement with the brand by 150 percent. These PWA load quicker and provide convenience for users as they travel. Customers appreciate that the PWA can help them load content faster and experience the convenience of engaging with the brand regardless of where they might be.

With a PWA, you can empower customers to easily make reservations, book opportunities with unique amenities, select packages or browse everything your hotel has to offer your guests directly from their browser. It will enhance their stay with you and help them feel more connected with what your hotel offers. With such an easy way to engage with your brand, customers will feel more attracted to what your business offers.

Employing search engine optimization (SEO)

As we explore building digital visibility, we can't neglect to discuss search engine optimization. Your website should employ SEO best practices for the hotel industry. This includes writing local-targeted content, which we will discuss in a moment, but also using essential strategies such as:

- Interlinking pages within your site
- Using strategic URLs that captured important keywords
- Researching the topics that matter to people visiting your area and addressing them in content
- Optimizing your images with keyword-rich Alt Text

Your SEO strategy needs to revolve around the audience you target with your hotel. Some hotels want to bring in travelers interested in luxurious experiences and others like the family-friendly crowd. One hotel might offer incredible wedding packages, while another has a strategic location between major tourist sites. Knowing what your audience wants to read about will help you build your keyword list, understand what content to create for your site, and help you structure your website to nurture interest.

There is another critical component of SEO that many hotels, unfortunately, overlook that I want to dive into with more detail.

Take advantage of schema opportunities

Although most businesses have already heard of and may practice the basics of SEO, many hotels overlook a vital component of this strategy that has the potential to highlight important aspects of your site: schema markup.

Schema is a structured data markup that Google uses to create unique results features. When results on the SERP go beyond the basic search results, such as highlighting a particular recipe or showing the number of stars a hotel is rated, it is thanks to the schema markup.

As a site owner, you want to know when using schema markup on your pages can significantly benefit your search visibility. For hotels, schema can play a variety of roles. Here are a few I want to draw your attention to:

1. Use schema markup for your hotel itself. Make sure Google registers that your web address is for a hotel business and includes details such as your contact information and address.
2. Employ the markup to help you highlight nearby events. If your hotel sponsors a special event, you can use the markup to bring it to Google's attention and get it highlighted in relevant searches.
3. You can use schema to highlight your hotel's room types and features.
4. You can add schema to your site to draw attention to your hotel restaurant, spa or other popular amenities that even non-guests might appreciate.

To research available schema markup, visit schema.org to get the markup you need and complete your business's information.

Employing the schema ensures that Google understands precisely the content you provide. You want Google to know that you are a hotel and what you have to offer people in your area. When opportunities for featured snippets appear in the SERP, you want your hotel website front and center. If people search for open hotel rooms directly on Google, you want the search engine to know that you have available rooms and communicate that to the potential customer. Schema markup means that your content is ready to take advantage of every opportunity on the SERP.

2. Incorporating your content marketing

Of course, we can't discuss building your visibility online without addressing the importance of content marketing and populating your website with high-value content that potential travelers want to read. A quality content marketing strategy for hotels will bring together three core components:

1. What you put on your website.
2. How you build visibility with social media.
3. How you use announcements and press releases to build your brand reputation and attract attention for your business.

Each side of this triangle tackles content slightly differently, but they come together to build an impressive online reputation for your organization. Let's start by exploring what you could be doing with your website.

Website content optimization

Travel is a highly visual industry. Customers don't want to book hotel rooms or excursions blindly—they rely on visuals like pictures and videos that let them know what they will get with a particular company. This means that your website has to incorporate these crucial visuals.

On your website, make sure you incorporate high-resolution photos that accurately depict what guests can expect when they stay in one of your rooms. You don't want to have a reputation for trickery by overusing photo editors to create an unrealistic image. At the same time, you want to use lighting, angles and arrangements to create appealing pictures that encourage people to stay at your hotel.

You then compliment your photos with location-based content. Forty-one percent of travelers say that location and activities play a significant role in how they make accommodation decisions. Therefore, use your content to help potential visitors see how you can help them tap into all that your region has to offer. Content that emphasizes your proximity to major sites, information about how you help your guests get to the major attractions and information about exploring your city will all help to bring traffic and visitors to your page. As we discussed earlier, search engines play a significant role as a resource for travelers as they make their travel plans. You want your website to be in the middle of it, encouraging customers to experience all they can in your local area.

Other significant factors for travelers making decisions are packages and offers. More than half of travelers say that deals impact their travel decisions and 21 percent specifically say that deals influence their accommodation decisions.

Therefore, constructing deals and packages that appeal to customers heading to your area can go a long way in drawing in visitors. However, to do this effectively, you need to make sure you fully understand what brings people to your hotel. Do they want to relax and rejuvenate? Then packages that focus on your spa and restaurant might help. If they're going to travel into your local city and spend their day on the go, then bundles with admissions passes and transportation to and from the sites can be a real draw. Construct packages that play to the interest of your customers.

Bring in your social media

In this age of mobile phones and social media, postings people make on the different social platforms play a significant role in travel plans and the popularity of destinations. Social media has begun to influence travel decisions across nearly all age groups. Half of Generation Z and Millennials, along with almost a third of Generation Y, say that Facebook influences their choices when booking a trip.

As a hotel, you want to tap into this source of information. Maintaining active social media pages where you create shareable material can help you make your destination appealing. Remember that to get people interested in staying at your hotel, you first need to attract them to your destination. Incorporate appealing pictures of your location into your social media strategy.

In addition to building a social media account with shareable images, you also want to encourage engagement on the page directly. Inviting customers to post user-generated content in your area or your hotel can be a great way to get started. You can host contests, create fun filters or otherwise entice people to participate.

You can also encourage more people to follow your pages using exclusive discounts. As people join your page, actively engage with them by answering their questions, inviting conversation and creating a community online. You can also share some of the content you produce on your website to draw more attention and traffic to your page.

You also want to keep social media in mind for your guests. With travelers so keen to take pictures for their own social media pages as they travel, look for opportunities to create a photogenic atmosphere for your guests. This user-generated content can help attract the followers of your guests.

As you create your social media strategy, you can also use it to post about local events that might attract travelers. For example, if your city hosts major sports tournaments or concerts, you can promote the upcoming event and let people know how your hotel can help them enjoy that event. Build your reputation as an integrated member of your community and a resource for people who enjoy participating in these local events. After the events, you can also post pictures from the event, particularly if your staff members attended. This can help you engage the wider community, further building brand reach.

Make announcements with press releases

The third prong of your content media strategy should be a periodic press release. With press releases, you can build attention and reputation for your hotel, letting potential guests know more about what has been going on with your hotel and what makes you an attractive place for travelers. The cornerstone of successful press releases is understanding your intended audience with the announcement. You want to reach travelers interested in your area, so you want an appealing title and approachable text to draw them in to learn more about you.

You can use press releases to announce a variety of different bits of news. For example, you might draft a press release to discuss hotel renovations, particularly if these renovations will add exciting new amenities or features. A press release like this can help to whet people's appetite for your hotel. You can share it on social media and on your website to encourage guests to learn more.

You can also use press releases to announce new team members. If the resort has new management that brings something exciting to the targeted travelers, let people know why they should care about this new leadership. If your hotel welcomes a new chef, let people know about their signature dishes and the tastes guests can explore at your hotel restaurant. Similarly, if your hotel will release some type of seasonal menu, let people know when you will start serving seasonal favorites.

Use the press release to encourage feelings of being one family among the staff. Building these bonds and getting people excited about the latest developments at your hotel will go a long way in attracting attention to your website and your digital branding efforts.

3. Bringing in local search

We also can't neglect to discuss the importance of local search when building your hotel brand online. People find hotels by doing local searches—they want to find a specific type of business within a particular area. Therefore, as you work to build visibility, your presence will need to capitalize on these local searches.

The cornerstone of local search is a Google Business Profile. We have already discussed how most travelers using search engines for their travel plans will turn to Google. Therefore, you can't underestimate the importance of a quality Google Business Profile page. If you have not already claimed your Google Business Profile page and completed your information, you should pause right now to get that done!

When people make local searches, Google will respond by delivering a carefully cultivated list of results for businesses in the vicinity indicated by the searcher. These results are pulled from the Google Business profiles. Google aims to list the companies that fill the query best, looking at a precise geographic location, ratings, and the amenities offered by the business.

Therefore, businesses should pay attention to their searches to appear in as many of these local-specific searches as possible. There are three essential areas you wish to pay attention to with your Google Business Profile page.

Listing Management

Let's begin by going over the fundamental principles of listing management on Google Business Profile.

One of the most important features you can nurture on your page is reviews. People looking at your business on this platform can easily see your star rating and read the reviews people have left for your hotel. Therefore, encouraging satisfied customers to leave reviews can play a significant role in your ability to build a positive impression on this platform. Additionally, as many as 72 percent of people say that they will leave a review if a business asks them to, so your efforts to cultivate reviews will not go to waste.

Make it easy for people to leave reviews while staying at your hotel. For example, you can include links to your profile page and in any communications from your hotel.

The other central component to managing your listing lies in the content you put on it. Make sure that you post various photos from all different angles showing rooms, amenities, your employees engaging with guests, and anything that expresses what makes your hotel different from the competition. Your pictures should be well lit and professionally taken to represent your business well.

You will also find that people often ask you questions through your Google Business Profile page. Regularly monitor this page to see the questions as they come in so you can answer them correctly and thoroughly. You don't want to overlook the importance of these questions.

Providing answers helps to demonstrate your attentiveness to your customers. You also never know when another potential customer might have that same question. Having a solution readily available can help improve people's confidence in your business.

If you see some of the same types of questions regularly pop up, you can also consider putting together FAQ pages. You can answer some of the most common questions you see to provide customers with quick resources on this type of page.

Optimizing Your Business Profile Page

In addition to the content you post on Google Business Profile, you also need to optimize your profile. You want your profile to show up on Google for as many searches as possible.

1. Make sure all your information is correct. Double-check details like your phone number and the hours listed.
2. Specify all your applicable attributes and amenities. If you allow dogs and someone searches for a dog-friendly hotel, you want Google to know that your hotel fits this criterion. Check off all your attributes such as parking, Wi-Fi, a pool and pet friendly. That is the only way to get Google to put your listing in the results.
3. Note any changes that apply to your hotel throughout the year. If you have certain changes that occur throughout the year—such as amenities only available in the summer—you should specify these changes on Google so they are clear to your customers.

Take your time filling out your profile so that the information represents your business as accurately as possible.

Pay Attention to Google Business Profile Posts

Finally, Google also allows users to use the Business Profile platform to make posts about their hotels. The key restriction is that Google does not want you to make announcements that promote upcoming events and sales that require people to click off to another site. Google wants people to explore the hotel through their own Google system.

As long as you keep this restriction in mind, however, you can use Google Business Profile to make a variety of important announcements. For example, you might draft a post about your COVID-19 precautions and the steps you take to protect guests' health. You might also let people know about upcoming happenings at the hotel or in your area. These posts can further engage potential guests and encourage them to learn more about what you have to offer.

4. Using Paid Search To Attract Clicks

Now that we have explored the efforts you can make to attract organic searchers, including SEO, content marketing and Google Business Profile, we will branch out into the paid side of building visibility.

To further build your visibility online, you can also turn to paid searches. Creating a paid search offers you the chance to bid and design ads that will get your hotel directly in front of interested customers. You will find several different types of paid ads available.

To begin, you can consider standard search ads. You place bids with an advertising platform like Google Ads for these text ads to appear when people search for particular terms on the search engine. For example, if someone searches for hotels in your area, you can bid to have your ad show up at the top of the screen.

Secondly, there are retargeting ads. Retargeting ads look for people who have engaged with your site previously but have not officially made a purchase.

For example, someone who visited your booking page but didn't book a stay might receive this type of ad as they browse online. You can design ads that remind people of what they left behind when they left your hotel site.

Finally, consider ads on social media platforms like Facebook and Instagram. These social media ads work a little bit differently than the ads that appear on search engine results pages. These ads target people based on specific demographics. For example, if you see people who like a particular type of music, and your city will have a music festival focused on that musical genre in a few weeks, you might target users like this person, creating an ad that entices them to come and attend the festival and stay at your hotel.

You can design a variety of different paid and promotional ads for your hotel. When you create one, make sure you customize it for the audience that will see it. For example, you might create display ads that target particular events your hotel intends to host. If you will serve as the site for a large luxurious wedding, see if you can get permission from the couple to use some footage of them and their guests in your ads. If you want to encourage tourists to local attractions, you can incorporate language and imagery that entices people to see the area.

Paid ads can play a variety of different roles as you work to build visibility. Some common usages include:

- Attracting attention to your site while you wait for organic rankings to improve
- Testing specific keywords and topics to see if the people searching for them will respond well to your site
- Highlighting essential events that you want to draw attention to but don't have time to wait for the organic listing to rise slowly
- Getting your hotel front and center for highly competitive keywords

All of this effort into the branded paid search world can be highly effective. CPC (Cost Per Click) advertising brings about 1 in 5 visitors to the hotel website. Creating an appealing promotion will help you get those visitors locked into the first step of a sales funnel—visiting your site and learning more about your hotel.

5. Exploring Analytics To Build Business

As you have followed these earlier steps, you have started to build a highly effective site and online presence that will serve your business well. It is not enough for customers to visit your hotel website; you want them to take specific actions such as booking a room. However, to effectively reach the peak of your business capabilities, testing, measuring and optimizing different parts of your site will help you better understand how customers respond to your hotel and where you have room for improvement.

Testing, Measuring & Optimizing

To understand how customers engage on your site, you need to have a strategy for effectively tracking and measuring the potential guests who land on your website. The first place to start is known as CRO testing (conversion rate optimization). With CRO, you analyze the number of people who follow your call to action. It provides you with greater insight into the behavior of customers, what they want from you, and how you can take steps to improve your ROI.

When you want to get started with CRO, use strategies such as A/B testing. Get started with the pages that have the most significant impact. As a hotel, these will likely be pages like your booking pages.

You want to test each part of your CTA so that you can gather the most precise data about what people respond to and where they most often land on your website. To run these tests, you need to have robust analytics in place. You will need to see how customers respond to two different types of CTAs (this is the A/B test). For your test to be effective, you need to be ready to question every assumption you have about customer behavior. Don't assume that certain words or colors will work best. As you gather more information, you will have more data about customer needs and behavior. This will give you information you can capitalize on to build your visibility further.

Your Tool For Measuring Progress: Google Analytics 4

In your arsenal for measuring your site progress will be Google Analytics 4. Google has announced that the previous version of Google Analytics has been shut down in 2023, making Analytics 4 your go-to tool for monitoring your traffic and tracking customers across platforms.

Google Analytics 4 is designed to track customers as they engage with your digital profiles across different platforms. It will help you analyze how people behave at different touchpoints and better understand how various aspects of your marketing strategy contribute to customer behaviors, such as booking a stay. This version of analytics will help you bring together both web and app event data for a complete picture of behavior online.

With Google Analytics you can gain valuable insight into how customers respond to your website and what actions they take. You can see, for example, how many people engage with your content about particular local attractions or events. You can see how much of this traffic then goes on to purchase bookings. With the improved ability to follow people across platforms and to understand attribution, you can see how different parts of your marketing efforts influence the eventual bookings people make.

Taking Hotel Marketing To The Next Level

Hotels have a reason to be excited. The travel industry has started to rise back up after a troublesome period during the pandemic. People have shown their interest in venturing back out and seeing new places to explore, relax and find entertainment. The opportunities are ripe for hotels to find new customers.

To attract these customers, you need to have a website and digital visibility to draw travelers browsing online.

Working with hotel digital marketing specialists can help you bring these different elements together. Experts in building SEO-first hotel websites can help you leverage all these opportunities offered. These experts can help you create highly targeted campaigns that will attract the attention you deserve and bring together all of the different elements of a well-optimized site. An experienced agency can help you leverage these opportunities and seize the changes coming for the hotel world.

Get ready to see what your hotel brand can do with the proper support. Position yourself for success as you embrace returning travelers.

Social Media Marketing

By Bruce Jordan MJ of Hotels (author)

A lot of hotels believe they can make a fortune on social media. And yes, it is possible. You can book a lot of reservations from social media. However, there's one thing that you need to have to make this happen organically. You need to have influence. And to be an influencer you need to get attention. Here are some popular platforms and this is why I use them, how I use them, and what I do with them.

Facebook

The first one is Facebook. Facebook is going to draw a mature crowd. Facebook is now officially titled Meta, but for some strange reason, they still use the term Facebook and so do all the people that use it. The number one thing about Facebook is that a majority of its users are mature people. And when I say mature, I mean people in the 30 to 60⁺ range are on Facebook. This is why it's such an amazing tool to use for your hotel. The first thing you want to do with Facebook is get local. Join a lot of the local groups so you can reshare their posts onto your page. Next thing you want to do is create a lot of videos and regular posts. It doesn't necessarily have to be about your hotel. It can be about anything that's going on in that town. But the most important things that you should post on Facebook are things to do in your area.

The next thing you need to understand is how to use hashtags. Most social media marketers try to use trending hashtags. But for hotels this may not be the best method unless you're already a part of that trend. The best 101 advice I can give for anyone in the hotel business when it comes to hashtags is always think local. When you're starting off, your hashtags should be searchable and using local hashtags keeps your post searchable to your target audience on every social media platform. If I live in Orlando my hashtags would consist of things that are close to me, things that are near me, and things to do that people are searching for parks, colleges, and events. Here are a few below as an example:

#Orlando
#LBV
#Downtownorlando
#UCF
#OrlandoMagic
#Kissimmee
#Downtownkissimmee
#Disney
#Universal
#Seaworld
#Orlandovacation
#orlandowedding

For more hashtags visit hotelrevenuebible.com/hashtags

When people come to your town or your location, they're always looking for things to do. So that's one of the first things that they're searching for. You should make sure that your post comes up in that feed when they're searching for it. The biggest mistake people make when using Facebook is they forget it's also a search engine. Always make sure the content you post is searchable. The first thing you want your future guest to see is your hotel, and your hotel posts. The best way to make sure your content is searchable is to add those things to do inside the keywords in your description (it also helps make sure the content is about that particular thing to do) whether it be a photo or video.

Quick sales tip, you can use Facebook and Instagram to search for hotel sales leads. When big groups like sporting events with teams and team players or group events are happening in the area or at your competitor's hotel, guests tend to do check-ins or even better, they take pictures and post or tag referencing your competitor's hotel on Facebook or Instagram to their post. Now if you just happen to be on your competitor's social media page for whatever reason (or follow the group's hashtag), you can see every "company" or "team" contact that took picture or made a post all in one place.

Instagram

Next is Instagram. I can't say Instagram is for the young crowd like Snapchat or TikTok. Instagram captures the 20 to 35ish crowd. And of course, some teens as well. This crowd is getting more mature and growing up in age. So they're more than likely going to be replaced by the Facebook crowd, some say within the next twenty years. Which is why it's so important to post on Instagram. What I love about Instagram is the reels. Even though Facebook has reels now, Instagram was the one to pioneer reels to compete with TikTok. Reels as of today are the in thing, but this may not be case later as the platforms algorithm changes.

Try to make as many reels as possible so that your videos end up in more potential guest feeds. Me, I tend to post on both. I will post Facebook reels and I will post my Instagram reels just to make sure I'm not missing any potential clients. Your strategy is pretty much going to be the same thing as Facebook, except I do a lot more tagging. I tag the stores that I'm promoting. I tag the person in my post when I'm reposting something that I found. But the most important advice I can give comes from Calvin Tilokee. Calvin is a social media influencer from Revparblems, you can find him on Instagram @revparblems. Here are some social media tips from Calvin.

Rule 1 – Don't make your social media page an extension of your website. The pictures on your website should be Photoshoped and/or very professional, the pictures on your social media page should not. When a guest sees something that looks too perfect, they tend to question its authenticity. Social media needs to look real and believable, try to keep your content as raw as possible.

Rule 2 – Make sure you have a strategy before you begin. You need to know your guest and what they are looking for, including (but not limited to) the type of guest you're trying to attract, the type of event business you want to bring into your hotel, and most important, you need to know your target market.

Rule 3 – Don't expect to make millions from one post. With social media you have to play the long game, it takes time and consistency to get the results you're looking for. You need to view social media as a part of your entire marketing strategy, not as a separate marketing tool.

LinkedIn

LinkedIn is amazing for sales; it's a great way to build connections and relationships in your community for potential prospects and leads. LinkedIn allows you to search by industry, location and even titles with a click of a button. LinkedIn is a fabulous way to get to know all of the business people in your target area without leaving your office. I tend to do a lot of connecting on LinkedIn when I am taking over a property in a different area that I'm not familiar with. It's a great sales tool, especially when you're prospecting for businesses in your area or ones coming to your area.

Here we are going to use one of three different scenarios in which you can use LinkedIn to gain more leads and more sales:

Parking Lot Shopping

Step one – **Getting the leads.** Parking lot shopping is when we go to your competition's hotel and look for business guests. We take pictures of the logos on the vehicles in the parking lot so we can later lure those businesses to your hotel. Once we obtain these logos, we simply input the company names into LinkedIn or Google to see if we can gain any additional contact information about them, this way we aren't flying blind during a prospecting sales call. I take it one step further by seeing if the company has a negotiated rate with the competition so I can use it in my pitch on LinkedIn. How do I get the competition's negotiated rate? I call the hotel and ask them for it, and they give it me. No joke, it's that simple.

Step two – **Connecting with the company.** Now that we have put the company names that we have gotten from our competitor's hotel parking lot into LinkedIn, it's time to start connecting. Never just connect

THE HOTEL REVENUE BIBLE

with one person in the company. Try to connect with as many people as possible. WHY? On LinkedIn, credibility is built with mutual connections. If someone sees that you share a mutual connection with them, especially if its within their company, it increases the chances of them accepting the invitation to connect from you versus declining the offer.

Step Three- **Connection Targets and Who to Pitch to**. Who will be the best person to pitch on LinkedIn? Most people will say the CEO, President, COO, or maybe a Vice President. Believe it or not it's the CFO or director of finance. For some strange reason, most finance people have never seen an expense they couldn't cut. Think about it. How many people in finance voted to increase their expenses (unless it's their own salary). Which is why you always start there with your value proposition (cost reduction offer) by directly messaging the head of finance first. Your message will look something like the following on LinkedIn.

"(Contact name) it was great connecting with, I notice that your company is overspending on lodging by 10% to 15%. Your current rate is XYZ with (competition hotel if you called to get their negotiated rate). I was hoping you could point me in the right direction to help me reduce this cost for you."

9 times out of 10 the person in finance will provide you with the direct contact you need to reduce this cost.

Step Four – **Call the contact**. If the finance department gives you the name of a contact you need to talk to, don't try to message that individual on LinkedIn. Call them directly and this is how you should begin that conversation ... "Hello (Decision Maker's Name) XYZ from the finance department told me to reach out to you to help you reduce the cost of your travel and lodging expenses. Right now, you're paying (hotel competition rate) per night. We thought it would be in your best interest to reduce this cost by 10% to 15% with (this rate). Do you have time for a site visit this week or the beginning of next week?"

Why does this work? 1) The decision maker automatically assumes that the person in the finance department knows about the reduction in the expense. The last thing someone wants to do is explain why we need to pay more money for an expense that can be reduced to the finance department. 2) The finance contact knows they can spend less money which means they are already on board and this gives you more leverage for them to change hotels, and 3) finally, you're not asking for a sale. You're just asking for a site visit, which gives you the opportunity to close a deal and/or at least add your hotel to their list as a second option.

This is only one of 3 scenarios, to learn more LinkedIn techniques go to hotelrevenuebible.com/linkedin.

YouTube

YouTube is one of the first places people go to when they're looking for videos about a spot they are planning to visit. YouTube is just starting to get into YouTube shorts to compete with TikTok but they're mainly known for long form videos. Not only do guests want to see what your hotel looks like, they also want to see what your hotel has to offer and the things to do in the area as well. On YouTube a possible guest is looking for someone else's opinion about your hotel with a video review. The guest is also looking for what your website doesn't say, they're looking for what your reviews don't say on issues your hotel maybe hiding. Most hotels post glitzy and glamorous pictures. On Youtube people are looking for the real deal and they want to know if the pictures may be better or worse than what you have online because it's harder to hide hotel imperfections in video form.

Your goal is to rank higher than every other hotel in your area for search and suggested videos in your area and beyond. For you to receive the result you want, you have to use focus keywords that your guests will be using when they type in their search. These are usually the same keywords they are searching for in Google. With YouTube, I always make sure I have a video for every single thing a traveling guest is searching for in my area. Keywords bring your videos traffic and with the right videos you will turn that video traffic into reservations.

Below is a list of all the videos you should consider making for your hotel's Youtube channel (only use the ones that apply):

Premier Video – your premier video should focus on the key elements of the hotel; it is designed to attract leisure guests. It should display and showcase all the features that make a guest feel at home. Smart TV, WIFI speed, USB ports, wireless chargers, bedding, pool, grill area, fire pit and major design features. The title should state your hotel name, the city and state it's in, I also try to use split titles (putting two titles into the title line) to gain better search results and search traffic. For example: Jordan Hotel Phoenix AZ | Best Hotel Near Phoenix AZ or use a destination that has a lot of search volume that is near your hotel. The purpose of this video is to increase leisure demand for your hotel and generate leads for sales.

School/College/University – If your hotel is near a school or college you want to make a video referencing that school or college and cross referencing your hotel in the video. This can be an informational video giving details about the school that just happens to display how far your hotel is located from the school or college. The purpose of this video is to increase demand for your hotel usually trying to capture the parents during major college events.

Hospital/Medical Center – This video will be the same as the college video except we will talk about the details of the hospital and how far the hospital is from the hotel. The purpose of this video is also to increase demand for your hotel.

Wedding Video – In the wedding video you want to show off the event space, the lobby area, and anything in your hotel that displays opulence. Record any and all features that are eye catching and engaging. Mix the video with photos to slow down the pace when necessary. Even if your hotel does not have enough event space for a wedding, you should still make a wedding video to let guests know they can create a group block to house the attendees. The purpose of the wedding video is to generate leads for sales.

Things To Do – You should make as many things to do videos as you can, the concept will be the same as the Hospital/Medical Center video. The purpose of this video is to increase leisure demand for your hotel.

Revenue Management Video Template – I always make three revenue management marketing videos. These videos are designed to increase demand on dates when demand is slow and it's time for a rate drop. Every revenue manager has 2 or 3 go to rates to help pickup rooms faster when their pace (room reservations) is slowing down. These videos will only be displayed or made visible when they need to be connected with a YouTube ad campaign.

Seasonal Events – you want to make a video about any event that comes to your area every year. Biking events, fairs, carnivals, sporting events, hunting seasons, car shows, etc. The purpose of these videos is to increase leisure demand for your hotel.

F&B – If you have F&B whether it be a free breakfast or full service with a couple restaurant outlets, you have to showcase your menu items to give the guest something to look forward to. There are three things that should be included in every F&B video 1. Drinks can be coffee, wine, or maybe a special drink from the bar. 2. Specialty Items a menu that is a best seller or a breakfast item that most guest love. 3. Happy People you must have happy people enjoying themselves eating and having a good time.

So, if they're searching for weddings, if they're searching for construction lodging, if they're searching for things to do, you need a video for that particular thing that they're searching for. You want your hotel to be first, I usually try to do 10 to 15 videos for a hotel if it's in a popular area, and five to 10 videos for a hotel if it's in a rural area. If you're in a rural area, you're not going to get as much search volume for your videos as if you would in a popular or more populated area.

But of course, you want to make sure that you're found organically. If you're a franchise, you have to use the franchise website, which can make things a bit more challenging to rank online, but much easier to rank on YouTube. If you're not a franchise, you must make sure that your YouTube page ranks very high in YouTube search and suggested video section.

TikTok

Next, we have TikTok. I have heard of hotels having huge success with TikTok. I just haven't seen that kind of success myself. However, you will probably get better results if you use influencers to promote your property on TikTok. Of course, it always pays to post content about things to do in your area and about your hotel. When people are searching for things to do in that area or searching for historical sites in that area, your hotel pops up from the hashtags and titles. You also have social media platforms like Snapchat and Pinterest and who knows how many others that will be coming in the future. I haven't had much success with TikTok, so I have just briefly mentioned it; perhaps you have a staff member who can be a rock star in this area and get your hotel noticed.

Putting It All Together

So, what do you do with all these platforms? One, know what hashtags to use and which ones are trending. The first thing I will do is when I create a post is use a local hashtag first. With Facebook you can use three or four hashtags without them slowing down your post. Instagram usually can take up to three also. LinkedIn, I use three to four hashtags and TikTok I use four or five, and for YouTube I use three hashtags to start. Never hashtag load your post (that is adding a bunch of hashtags to your post) because most platforms will slow your post down and reduce your reach (the number of people that see your post). The second thing I would do is find the hashtags for the places that my guests are coming from. If your guests are coming from Miami, I would use local hashtags in the Miami area in my post to market to the Miami area.

For instance, in Orlando, we get a lot of traffic from Jacksonville, Miami, and Palm Beach. So, I create social media content and find local hashtags for those areas. My posts will pop up and hopefully inspire a vacation or two back to my hotel in Disney World, Universal or SeaWorld. This will be a little different for your market. But this is one of the main things that you want to focus on in local hashtags, the best way to find out where your customers are coming from is to download your database from your PMS system. When you download your database into an Excel spreadsheet, they can be sorted by city, state, and zip code and that's the easiest way to find out where your guests are coming from.

Is your hotel running a little slow on the weekends or on certain days? You can run a promotional rate for those days and market that rate directly to the consumer. You can offer a bigger discount because you won't have to pay any OTA fees (Online Travel Agent fees) for the days you're trying to increase occupancy. If you're going to give a discount, give it to the guest that wants to book directly with you. Let them know you appreciate their loyalty.

Creating Content

When most people think about content creation, the 1st thing they do is try to hire a production team … which is great if you have the budget for it. But for some small hotels they believe they just can't afford the type of content they want to create and so don't do anything. For most people they believe they would rather have quality content or nothing at all and this is a mistake. I would rather have average content verse no content. Most people start off with a cellphone that takes decent pictures and videos. Everybody wants their pictures and videos to be the best of the best. Unfortunately for most people, they don't have the Hollywood studio equipment to make something like that happen. The first thing you want to start with is an amazing smartphone. Find out which employee has the best phone and use their phone to start taking pictures and videos.

This will at least get you started in the right direction until you can do something to upgrade the quality of your digital presence. First start taking pictures and videos of the good things that the guests like the most. The bed, the TV, breakfast items, especially their favorite, get close ups. Don't be scared, make a video with your cellphone or hire video editors. Don't be scared to hire a photo editor. There are some photo editors that edit a photo for as little as $1.00 a picture, it's worth the investment. You can hire someone at www.fiverr.com/pe/5pj8mk .

Most importantly, don't be afraid to repost your content. The main purpose of social media is not just to make content and sell rooms, it is to make sure that your guests never forget about you. To make sure you're at the top of your guests' mind so they can always remember the experience that they had at your hotel is the goal. This way, you'll be the first person (or place) they're thinking about when it's time to rebook.

Going into the next chapter there are four terms you'll need to understand. Reach, impressions, frequency, and engagement. Let's break each one down.

Reach - represents the number of unique users who see your post or page (regardless of whether they've engaged with it). Let's say you publish a post and 100 people look at it. Your reach is 100 people.

Impressions - the number of times any content from your page or about your page entered a person's screen. Your reach can be 100 but your impressions can be 200 because some people may have seen the same post or page twice.

Frequency - the average number of times each person saw your ad. This will give you a better breakdown of the true number of impressions your post is getting. Let's say my reach is 100, my impressions are 300, and my frequency is 3.0. This means my post or page was seen by 100 people (reach), 300 times (impressions), and the same 100 people seen my post 3 times (3.0 frequency).

Engagement - all of the ways that users can interact with your content—through likes, comments, shares, saves, etc.

Hotel Ad Campaigns

By Bruce Jordan MJ of Hotels (author)

Now it's time to talk about everybody's favorite subject: hotel ad campaigns. You can run different hotel ad campaigns with different platforms like Google, YouTube, Microsoft Bing, Instagram, Facebook, TikTok, so on and so forth. It is a science and an art. Running an ad campaign is something that if you don't know how to control it, you can lose a lot of money fast. For some people, it's worse than gambling. Today, we're going to give you the foundation that you need to get started. How much to spend is usually everyone's number one question.

As a common rule, I usually use a percentage of my transit revenue to calculate what my ad spend should be for the month. For some hotels, it's 1% to 2% of revenue. For other hotels, it's three to five percent especially if you're a boutique hotel. Boutique hotels usually spend a lot more on ads than franchise hotels. The reason is all the money that they're saving from franchise fees, they must reinvest in branding, marketing and advertising. If nobody knows you, they can't stay with you at your hotel.

Before we begin there are a couple of terms you'll need to know which are CPC Cost Per Click, Click Through Rate, Placement, Audience, Campaign, Ad Group, Relevance Score, Conversion Rate

CPC (Cost Per Click) - is a metric that determines how much advertisers pay for the ads they place on websites or social media, based on the number of clicks the ad receives.

CTR (Click Through Rate) - is the number of clicks that your ad receives divided by the number of times your ad is shown; clicks ÷ impressions = CTR

Placement - the group of ad units where advertisers can place ads.

Audience - a group of people identified as likely customers of a business.

Campaign - a set of advertisements that work together to promote a product or service.

Ad Group - contains one or more ads that share similar targets.

Relevance Score - calculated based on the positive and negative feedback we expect an ad to receive from its target audience.

Conversion Rate - measures the number of users who converted as a percentage of the total number of users that visited your site.

CPM - cost per mille, which means cost per thousand impressions

Type of Campaigns

There are generally six to seven types of campaigns I use to increase occupancy and revenues for the hotels I manage. Most are for offense, a few are for defense.

1. **Competition campaign** – a competition campaign is designed to swipe your guests away from the competition. This can be done through Google, Facebook, YouTube, Microsoft Bing etc.

2. **Revenue campaign** - This is designed for people that are searching for hotels in your area for a place to stay. The revenue campaign will drive that traffic to your website using search terms like "things to do in (town)," "hotels near (town) and (location)." People are looking for things to do in your area, which is probably the reason why they're traveling there. So you want to make sure you have ads running when it comes to the things to do in that area. If they're coming to do those things, they're going to need a place to stay after they finish. And you want your hotel to be first in line.

3. **Sales campaign** - The difference between a revenue campaign and a sales campaign is that a sales campaign is designed to generate leads for group business like weddings, funerals, events, sweet sixteens and so on. These are purpose driven campaigns to get larger businesses and larger groups through the door. Whether it be video or Google search, they're specifically designed for sales.

4. **Protection campaigns** – these campaigns are designed to protect and defend you from entities that are running competition campaigns against you.

5. **Revenue management campaign** – these campaigns are designed to increase bookings on dates that revenues are slow and you need to pick up the pace and generate more occupancy.

6. **Retargeting campaigns** – these campaigns are designed to retarget guests that have already stayed at your hotel or retarget potential customers that have engaged with your content.

7. **Lookalike campaigns** – these campaigns are designed to target similar potential customers, or should I say the customers or guests that are close to your ideal buyer's persona, when running ads.

Competition Campaign Strategy

Google Ads Search, Microsoft Bing, and YouTube are some of the platforms you can use to run paid search ads. As stated, the goal of the competition campaign is to take potential guest away from your competition. Step one, make a list of all the top performing hotels in your market segment and/or area. You can get this information with a Google search or by going to TripAdvisor. Step two, create a search campaign in Google Ads and Microsoft Bing and create a video campaign in Google Ads for YouTube. Step three, add the names of your competitors' hotels to your campaign under keyword search. The result is that when someone searches for your competitor's hotel, *your* property's advertisement should pop up which will give you a chance to takeaway business from your competitor.

Revenue Campaign

Google Ads Search, Microsoft Bing and Youtube will be the platforms you can choose to run these paid ads. Step one, make a list of all the things to do in the area where your hotel is located. Step two, create a search campaign in Google Ads and Microsoft Bing and create a video campaign in Google Ads for YouTube. Step three, add the list of the things to do and local keywords including the following keywords to your keyword search column "hotel in (your city)," "hotel near (your city)," "hotels near (landmarks in your area)," etc. The result is that when someone searches for things to do or hotels in your area, your hotel's advertisement should show up on the first page/screen of results.

Sales Campaign

Google Ads Search, Microsoft Bing, Youtube and Facebook will be the platforms for these ads. Step one, make a list of all the wedding venues, event venues, funeral homes, top business firms, and events in your area. Step two, create a search campaign Google Ads and Microsoft Bing (create a separate search campaign for events like concerts and end the campaign after the event is over). Step three, create a separate video campaign for each category in Google Ads. Step four, add your keywords for the event venues, wedding venues, and top business firms in your area. Step five, create a Facebook campaign and create an audience for people looking for weddings, event venues, events, and the top business firms. Step six, create a Facebook campaign and add that audience to your campaign as your target audience. The result is that when someone searches for weddings or events in your area your hotel advertisement should pop up.

Protection Campaign

Google Ads Seach, Microsoft Bing and YouTube will be the platforms for these ads. Step one, make a list of all the different ways a guest may search for your hotels name or enter your hotel's name in Google Search. Step two, create a search campaign Google Ads and Microsoft Bing. Step three, create a separate video campaign for your hotel using your premier video in Google Ads. Step four, add the list of names in the keyword section for your campaigns.

Revenue Management Campaign

Google Ads Search, Microsoft Bing, YouTube and Facebook will be the platforms for these ads. Step one, select the rate you want to market to potential customers. Step two, create a search campaign in Google Ads and Microsoft Bing using your rate in the search ad. Step three, create a video ad campaign in Facebook and YouTube using a video with the rate you want to market. Step four, choose a broad location and a broad audience. Step five, if your reservations aren't picking up for that day, retarget the same audience with over 10 second watch time with a lower rate using a different video.

Retargeting Campaigns

YouTube and Facebook will be the platforms for these ads. Step one, download a list your guest from your PMS system which should include first and last name, phone number and most important their email address. Step two, create an audience and upload the list from your PMS into Facebook and YouTube. Step three, use this audience as your target audience when running your campaigns and ads.

Lookalike Campaigns

Facebook will be the platform for these ads. Step one, download a list of your guest from your PMS system which should include the first and last name, phone number and most important their email address. Step two, create an audience and upload the list from your PMS into Facebook. Step three, with the audience you just created, create a lookalike audience and test at 1% to 3%.

Reducing Ad Spend & Ad Cost

The next thing we can do to get our costs down is target the correct areas with our campaigns. Focus on targeting people in a particular area that guests are coming from. Most of us know where our guests are coming from, find a pattern, then create ads to target people in those areas and zip codes. If you don't know where your guests are coming from the easiest way to get this data is to download your guest list into excel from your PMS system and sort by city, state, and zip code.

Sometime there are websites that can generate a lot of traffic and reservations for your hotel, but they don't participate in Google Ads. In cases like these it's better to go straight to the source. Websites like movingtoflorida.com, real estate websites in your area, hospitals nearby and/or local popular things to do websites in the area are great sources. The best way to find these websites to advertise on is to do a simple Google search and find out how much traffic the website is producing to see if it's worth advertising on. To get this information, copy and paste the website URL into spyfu.com which will give you the website traffic stats and the top-ranking website keywords. Next, get in touch with the website admin and make them a CPC (cost per click) or CPM (cost per 1,000 impression) offer.

Sometimes contacting the websites directly comes out a little bit cheaper than running ads through Google, Taboola or the like. Now the most popular place, of course, is going to be Google Search ads. These are the ads that you see at the top of the screen when someone is searching for a specific topic. For instance, if someone is searching for hotels in a certain city, you want to be at the top of the list. The problem is this sometimes gets a little expensive depending on your market, where you're located, and how much the keywords are going for.

So the best thing you can do is set a minimum budget for the main keywords and set a maximum budget for similar keywords or long tail keywords to save money. When people travel, they're looking to travel to a location and they're looking to be near something or close to something that they're traveling to. Most of the top search terms are hotel near (name of the hospital near you), hotel near (name of the town you're in), hotel near a (name of the college near you), hotel near (name of the a funeral home your near), hotel near (name of the things to do in your area). You want to make sure you put these in your top keywords when you're running Google Search ads and setting up ad campaigns.

The next thing that will reduce your ad cost is using the right keywords. If you are running a search ad campaign or creating a website that you want to rank higher on search engines like Google, you have to know what keywords will work well for you in your market. There are a couple simple easy ways to find keywords to use on your website and search campaigns. Strategy number one will be taking them from your competition. Go to your competitor's website like a popular boutique hotel in the area, copy and paste the URL in spyfu.com. This should give you the website traffic and top keywords your competitor is ranking for. Next, find the monthly search volume for those keywords and the cost to use them in a campaign. You can get this information from Google Ads, for me it's easier to view in a web browser extension called Keywords Everywhere. The extension will show me all the data metrics and estimated cost for keywords I am researching during a search.

Reducing ad costs for Facebook is a little bit different than for Google ads. With Facebook, there's a couple of things that you must consider in order to know if your ads are performing well. Facebook and Instagram ads can be run from the same platform through Facebook Ads Manager. When reviewing your ad's performance, things that you see most when you're looking at Facebook ads are going to be reach, impressions, frequency, link clicks, cost per click, video plays, and video average time plays.

Here is another quick breakdown: reach is the number of people that are seeing your ad, impressions are the number times they see it, frequency is how often the same person is seeing your ad. If your frequency rate is at 3.0, that means the same person has seen that same ad three times. The link clicks lets you know how many people have clicked on that ad, and the cost per click will let you know how much it is costing you for each click. Video plays let you know how many times the video has been played or been seen. Video average play time is the most important because this determines how effective and engaging your video is for that campaign. The standard time is three seconds. The higher the video play time, the more effective your campaign is because it's actually capturing the individual's attention so they want to see and know more. The best way to reduce costs with Facebook ads is to stay current with the type of content guests are consuming in the correct format. What type of content should you post? I do a lot of videos. But most importantly, I also do reels. At the writing of this book reels are extremely popular and it seems like the algorithm is giving you an incentive to do Facebook Reels.

Google Hotel Ads

Now let's move on to Google Hotel ads. Google has gotten into the travel game with their Hotel ads. Google Hotel ads is something that is different and separate from Google ads. I use both; I use Google ads for my YouTube ads, my instream YouTube ads, I use them for my search ads, my YouTube search ads. And of course, I use them for my regular Google ads for Google Search. The number one reason I use Google Hotel Ads is because that's where the OTAs are. They are bidding aggressively to get business from Google, right on your own Google My Business page listing. This is the way it works. You go to Google; you create a business profile on Google for your hotel (if you don't already have one). Then the OTAs can bid on the profile that you created to get the business from your profile on to their website.

On top of the OTAs, they're SEO masters (also most are good as the MJ of Hotels). So, you really, really, really want to pay attention to Google Hotel Ads. There's two ways that you can get your bids, listings, and rates on your own Google profile with Google Hotel Ads. One of them is, of course, you have an approved channel manager that will submit the meta data to Google, better known as a certified integration partner. The other one is a little bit more technical, and you're more than likely you're going to have to hire a coder. Because Google Hotel Ads require a direct feed to your hotel's rates and inventory via your CRS or booking engine. And it's going to be a very, very, very manual process. Personally, I recommend you go ahead and get an approved channel manager. Most of the top channel managers are approved for Google Hotel Ads including a Channel Manager called Roadrunner.

The second thing you're going to plan is your ad cost strategy. How do you set your ad cost strategy so you don't go bankrupt trying to compete with other OTAs on your own listing. There are two different types of programs you can choose for Google Hotel ads as of the writing of this book. One is a Commission per stay (CPS) model and the second one is a Commission per acquisition (CPA) model, which means that you set a budget for the amount that you're willing to pay for each reservation per night with a max bid.

It's easier to control the CPS because that is based on bookings. CPA is not so easy. And now you have one more thing to consider in your strategy equation: click bait. A lot of new and upcoming OTAs know they can't compete with the bigger ones. They know they can't compete with you on pricing, but they need traffic to their site; so they will mislead potential guests and make up fake lower rates that they know are not legit. Then a person will click on this extremely low rate (click bait) thinking they're getting a better deal. By the time the guest gets to the checkout page, they get hit with fees that they would never have paid had they booked with the hotel directly. So that's something else that you must take into consideration as well.

I always recommend people use a CPS model. And once they develop their skills and they know their market well enough, then they can start using a CPA model. This is why the CPS model is only going to be a percentage of revenue for the entire guest stay, and you only pay if the guest completes the reservation. So if Google charges 5%, 10%, or 15% of revenue as a commission, you don't lose because if a guest cancels or no shows you just submit a cancelation report to Google. The commission percentages with Google have been going up, so please keep that in mind.

TIP: if I have a seven-day reservation, paying a 10% commission, it's going to be 10% per night. The good news is, if I get the guest to extend in house, all the additional revenue from the date of extension is non-commissionable, I don't have to go back to Google and report to them the guests that they sent me spent another night.

When it comes to CPA, once you know your market, a CPA model will actually save you a lot of money because you know what you want to spend, you know your seasons, you know your traffic, you know your analytics. Until you know all that information, I don't recommend a CPA model. Like anything else, you can run out of money fast with a CPA model. The best way to keep from going bankrupt when you're doing this is to make sure that you set up a conversion tracker on your website. Setup a conversion tracker on the page that your guests' land on after they finished completing a purchase. This is usually the thank you page or confirmation page.

The purpose of the conversion tracker is so you know how many sales you are receiving from your Google Hotel ads. If a guest clicks on an ad and makes a purchase, that counts as one conversion. So, let's say if you have 10 clicks and only one person made a purchase, that's a 10% conversion rate. Please keep track of your conversion rates because it lets you know how effectively your ads are performing. It also lets you know how effective your bidding model is and if you need to change your bidding strategy. This is extremely important, especially for boutique hotels that don't have a huge marketing budget.

The Downside of Google Hotel Ads

No Keyword targeting - Unlike standard paid search campaigns, there is no keyword targeting option associated with a Google Hotel ads campaigns. You're limited to geographic targeting, some different bid modifier options and 1st part audience targeting options. This is why I use both Google ads and Google Hotel ads

No In-market or Affinity Audiences - Google Hotel ads only give you the option to target/exclude your 1st party audience lists.

Rate Parity – The more competitive your rate is and in-line with the other OTA rates, the lower your ad cost will be on the platform. Which means if you set your rate high on your own website and lower with the OTAs, your ad cost could increase. This explains why some franchises are starting to penalize franchisees for rate parity violations. I see some as high as $250 per violation.

The MJ of Hotels 3 Point Shot

When running Google ads, the one thing that you need to be careful with is your relevance score. A bad relevance score could increase your ad cost and slow down your impressions, which means it will cost you more money to deliver fewer ads. Make sure you try to maximize your click through rate to avoid this from happening.

Email Marketing

By Bruce Jordan MJ of Hotels (author)

You know, most hotels get email marketing so confused. And they make it very complicated when it really doesn't have to be. The purpose of email marketing is to:

1. Brand your hotel.
2. Keep customers engaged with your hotel.
3. Make guests an exclusive special offer for being a loyal customer.
4. Generate demand for slow dates that aren't picking up as fast.
5. Maintain your relationship with your customer.

Brand Your Hotel

Emailing shouldn't just be for surveys; it should also be used as a tool to help hotel guests get the word out and share their experience with their friends. When you email a survey, also include a link to your Google My Business review page or TripAdvisor page so the guest can leave a review if they a had a good experience.

Keep Customers Engaged

Let guests know of any changes that may happen to your hotel. New menu items or specials that your restaurant may have. Allow guests to vote on different changes you are thinking about making to the hotel. Let's say you want to change a menu item at breakfast like cereal. Let the guest vote on it. Set up an account at surveymonkey.com and email them a link to voting page. People who are given a voice usually stay committed to the organization that gave them a choice.

Exclusive Special Offers

The next thing that you need to capitalize on is email offers. People use emails to make offers that they would not traditionally advertise on an OTA site. The great thing about email marketing is that it gives you an advantage. It gives you control because you have a direct connection to a guest, which is why you should always have your front desk staff collecting real email address from guests who used third party booking sites. Pay the commission once to get the guest, keep the guest booking directly with email offers to lower commissions.

So, what do you offer? The three main things most travelers want are status, an experience, and exclusivity. A status offer is offering a room with a special view, pool view, ocean view, and/or a suite at a special rate that is unavailable to regular guests. An experience offer is offering a package with tickets included for a sporting event, things to do or other special events. An exclusivity offer is offering premium amenities like a VIP section of the pool with extended hours. When it's time to get heads in beds you must get creative.

Generate Demand

Let's talk about generating demand for your hotel. There was a reason why a new guest came to your hotel. For most guests the number one reason was location. Nine times out of ten there's something going on in your area that is either going to bring them back, or simply something familiar about the area that makes them want to return. It could be friends and family, it could be events, or most importantly, it could be things to do.

When we are preparing emails to generate demand, we want to send more emails about things to do and/or any events that are coming to town than they may be interested in, instead of shoving a bunch of offers and discounts down their throat. In addition, tell them why they need to come back to the area before you tell them how cost-effective their return will be. If your hotel has a lot of sporting events, that should be the content that goes inside your email campaign in the following format: Date of the event, Name of the Event, Event Time, and Special Rate for Event/Returning Customer.

Maintain Relationships

This seems like the easiest thing in the world, but most hotels drop the ball on this one all the time. Send out birthday emails, holiday emails and anniversary emails to your guests. These relationships are easy to maintain and can be set up to go out automatically every year without fail.

Maintaining Your Email List

There are a couple things we must do to maintain our email list so that emails flow smoothly and are less time consuming. First thing we must do is run all the new emails we are adding to our email campaign platform through a bounce checker to make sure the email is valid. Guests make mistakes and most importantly the front desk makes mistakes and from time to time you'll get a typo here and there that will cause the email to bounce. Bounced emails tend to trigger red flags and look like spam to an email campaign platform.

Next, you should always tag your email so that they are easier to sort when you want to use them for different types of campaigns. For instance, I wouldn't want to send a branding email to someone in my birthday campaign. I can avoid this by tagging my emails. Finally, you want to choose an email marketing platform. For a list of email marketing platforms go to hotelrevenuebible.com/email

Why Email Marketing

If I send an email and get a returning guest, it costs me nothing except an email. With email marketing, your message is key. I tell people it may be best to hire a copywriter. Hire someone that can write the scripts for these emails, this way you're not getting people that are just saying the same old message such as "this is what is in town get 10% off, come down and give me your money."

Best Time to Send Emails

What is the best time to send emails? It depends on the type of traveler that you're looking to attract. If most of your hotel guests are business transient, I would schedule your email campaign to go out first thing in the morning between five and six AM. This way it will be the first thing they see in their inbox. If you're looking for a leisure traveler, I would schedule the emails to go out around lunchtime, because most people tend to go on their phones around lunchtime or late evening between seven and nine o'clock PM.

This way, they'll get the email when they're on the phone. Business people open up and read emails all day long. People that are using their personal time to be on their phone are going to be the ones that will open emails sporadically throughout the day or after they finish work. So that will be the best time to send emails to that target audience. The most important part and thing to focus on is going to be the headline (subject line), you want the headliner to scream: open me!

What tends to get people to open emails faster for hotels, and have a better open rate, is a news related headline. If you're sending an email about things to do, or events going on in the area, you should generalize your headline around that topic. Most hotels send the same email every month that usually reads something like this: Oh, hey, open me get a 20% discount. The headline needs to state why the person should be interested in the email in the first place. If they have no interest in your topic, they're not going to open the email. So that's the first thing we must focus on: the topic that attracts their attention.

Finally, with email marketing, you want to focus on the analytics, keep an eye on your open rate and click through rate. The average open rate for an email campaign is around twenty-two percent. If you have a low open rate revisit your subject line and rethink your headliner. The average click through rate is between one and two percent. If your click-through rate falls below this rate it may be time to find a new copywriter. For more information about emails visit hotelrevenuebible. com/email

How To Save Revenue

By Bruce Jordan MJ of Hotels (author)

I don't see the point of making a bunch of revenue, just to lose it. So we're going to talk about some of the things that you want to look out for and things you need to do to make sure you don't lose the revenue that you've generated. First thing, first: cancellations.

Yes, guests who want to cancel. Some guests want to cancel when they're outside of the cancellation policy timeline, and some guests want to cancel when they are inside of the cancellation period. We need to make sure that we're training our front desk staff to save revenue as well as discouraging the guest from canceling. Whether they're inside or outside the cancellation policy, the first thing you need to do is find out why do they want to cancel. A lot of times they want to cancel because their event got canceled or rescheduled. The first thing we need to offer them is to reschedule the reservation versus just straight out canceling it. Most guests don't know they have this option, which becomes a little more difficult when they book on OTA websites like booking.com, Expedia, Agoda, or other 3rd party websites. So that should be your first offer: reschedule the guest reservation for a different date.

Your second offer should be a discounted rate. This is very different for someone that is not prepaid versus someone who is prepaid. When there is a prepaid reservation, the guest can't cancel anyway, so it's not an issue. For someone who's not prepaid, we should be able to offer them the prepaid rate to save the reservation. It takes a lot of time, work, and effort to get the guests to our hotel. By allowing a cancellation, all your marketing dollars and everything else go down the drain. Give your front desk agents a little more leeway to negotiate a better rate to stop a cancellation.

The third thing is no shows. Guests no show all the time. If they don't want to be charged, they should get the same offer to reschedule. We can reschedule their reservation; it will be prepaid and nontransferable, especially if they are repeat guests. This way you don't have to worry about them trying to dispute the charge with their credit card company. If you offer them a different date, specify that they can't cancel or can't get refunded. Most guests are more than willing to accept a new date for their reservation.

The next area where hotels lose a lot of revenue is with declined credit cards when reserving a room for guests. We don't know if they're coming or not. They don't show and their credit card declines when we try to charge them for a no-show charge. So now we don't have any recourse for the no show even though we have a room that we could have sold. This always happens when you're almost sold out. We have a room, but we can't charge the credit card, so we get screwed in the end.

The best thing to do is to check the card as soon as the guest is within the cancellation policy, try to authorize the card for one night room tax. If the credit card declines, we reach out to the guests, let them know that their card declined. Let the guest know we need a valid form of payment before we can proceed with the reservation and ask for another card. If we can't get in contact with the guests, it's just best to cancel a reservation. You don't want to hold a reservation for declined credit card; from my experience, a credit card declining is usually going to be a problem.

Finally, we are going to cover issuing refunds. The rate should not be the last thing that you refund. There's a series of other things that you can offer a guest besides a refund to compensate them for any issues that they have with their stay. I can offer a guest a refund on something else, like a pet fee, or an upgrade fee, or something of that nature before I offer them a refund of the revenue generated from the room rate. I can offer gift cards or reward points or something of that nature before offering them a refund on the rate. The reason why I don't like offering refunds on a rate is because it messes with your ADR. You're reducing your ADR for no reason. In addition, some guests don't see a refund as a remedy, the average guest just wants their problem solved.

But there are some scam artists out there that believe they're entitled to a full refund and all their money back because the flowers were too big on the trees outside. That's just a give in. Unfortunately, this was created by us for us by allowing these types of refunds to guests for any and every little thing that they find. So, I get it. You're going to have to issue refunds from time to time but the last thing you want to do is issue a refund on the rate if possible. These are some of the top ways to make sure we are saving revenue.

How To Find Lost Revenue

By Bruce Jordan MJ of Hotels (author)

Now we're going to talk about how to find lost revenue that you didn't even know you had. There's revenue on your books, you got the payment for it. But probably didn't post the revenue or record it inside the system or vice versa. You recorded the revenue but didn't get the payment. So today we're going to be talking about how to find lost revenue and where to look for it.

Cancellation Reports

Every system is different. Some of this may apply, just in different ways than your system may do it; so make sure you understand the concept and then find out how to make it work in your hotel. On your cancellation report, you have a lot of people that have prepaid reservations, and when they cancel the payment gets recorded but sometimes the front desk forgets to post the revenue, or the system is down and it never fully is recorded. So that revenue stays in the advanced deposit ledger. For days, weeks, months, I've even seen years, a cancellation report can show all prepaid deposits taken but none of the revenue was recorded.

You want to review your cancellation report every day. Make it part of your nightly audit process; check the cancellation report and post any advance deposits pertaining to those reservations.

No Show Report

The no show report is key for me, because my hotels take payment in advance just in case the guests don't show up. The payment for the first night's room and tax is already posted so the no show penalty is secured. But a lot of times at other hotels a guest will no show and the front desk or night audit forgets to post the room and tax, or they may forget to take the payment. If a guest doesn't show up, sometimes they never get charged. And after a while the guest thinks that they're safe. Then someone like me comes along and says, "Hey buddy, you owe us this amount." To prevent this, add this process to your nightly audit so staff will always make sure the revenue is posted and the hotel has collected payment.

Guest Ledger

The guest ledger is very important and should be audited every day. With the guest ledger you want to look for guests that are past their checkout date that still have a balance. If a guest has a positive balance this means that room and tax has been posted but the payment hasn't been collected. If the guest has a negative balance this means payment was collected, but room and tax haven't been posted. The guest ledger should be reviewed every night, either by management or night audit staff to make sure you're not losing revenue or missing payments.

Miscellaneous Income

Make sure you check Miscellaneous Income on a monthly basis. I'm talking about third party income like laundry machines, vending machines, soda machines, and ATM machines. Call the vendor and ask them for a detailed sales report, plus a breakdown of the commissions to show the commissions you're getting. Make sure that you actually get your share. There are many times I walked into a new management contract for a hotel, and I saw large vending machines, candy machines, ATM machines, and that hotel hadn't received their commission in years. I called the vendors and got them a huge lump sum check. Make sure you're always crossing your Is and dotting your Ts and running those commissions through your PMS system. This way it will be easier to track missing payments.

Hotel F&B

By Bruce Jordan MJ of Hotels (author)

For food and beverage revenue, the days of waiting for occupancy or depending on hotel occupancy are long gone. In today's game, your restaurant must survive and stand on its own. It must be able to stand on its own two feet and bring in a profit. A lot of hotel management companies or hotel owners believe that restaurants are an additional expense. Well, it will be if you don't know how to market and sell the restaurant properly. Like any business, the first thing a restaurant needs is traffic. The best way to get more traffic is to separate your restaurant from your hotel, even though it's in the same building. The restaurant should have its own Google My Business listing, it should have its own Trip Advisor Listing as well. By separating the two, the restaurant stands on its own and won't be viewed as just another hotel restaurant.

The other thing that you'll see by separating the two is that it separates the reviews. If someone has a bad experience in the restaurant, it doesn't go on to your hotel reviews. And if someone has a bad experience in the hotel, it doesn't go on the restaurant reviews. By separating the listings from the hotel and the restaurant, you are separating the potential of having a decreased review score because of what went wrong inside the restaurant.

Getting More Restaurant Traffic

The way your restaurants can get more attractive traffic is by advertising throughout the hotel. The first person that should be advertising the restaurant is the front desk at check-in. In their check-in spiel, they should be mentioning your restaurant, the hours of operation, and their favorite dish (best for owners if it is a high priced item). This way you maximize your profit. Next, you want to offer free drinks to get them into the restaurant. I see a lot of hotels that offer free wine or free beer or something of that nature at check in. There's nothing wrong with that. But if your hotel has a restaurant, you're literally taking business away from the restaurant because they're just going to take the drink and go back to the room. By doing this, you are missing the main goal.

Most importantly, when you're giving out free drinks make sure it's one drink per room to entice them to buy the next drink. Especially when couples are coming in together. They're not just going to let one person drink by themselves. When you give out one drink per room, the other person is going to want to buy a drink.

Next there should be pictures and menu items on elevators, in the fitness center, and in pool areas. Close and near to the front desk there should be displays of pictures of your top selling food items or your food items that generate the most revenue at the lowest food costs. A lot of times I like to sacrifice my S&P budget just to bring traffic into the restaurant.

Next thing is how to create demand for the restaurant. Number one, events and live entertainment.

Everyone loves live entertainment. If you have the space and the budget to bring in some live entertainment (live band, live DJ or artists that have a decent following) that will be your number one take. It doesn't necessarily have to be an out-of-pocket expense. There are some bands and DJs that will take a cut from the bar or a percentage of sales from the bar for the time that they're doing their set. Another way to bring traffic into the restaurant is from Uber Eats. Uber Eats, Doordash, Grubhub and the like will bring in more traffic. You don't have to wonder if your kitchen is going to stay busy, those platforms will keep your cooks busy. The only thing I don't like about the Uber Eats, Door Dash, and Grubhub's of the world is that they're cut is sometimes just a little too high for good profits. Which is why you must start promoting locally.

Promoting Locally

Promoting locally is not the easiest thing in the world to do. The best way to promote locally is to hire influencers to come and review your restaurant. And I'm not talking about any old average influencer, I mean some powerful influencers that had a decent local following to record a video review of your restaurant. Some of them will come and review it for just a free meal. Others will come and review it for a couple hundred dollars. Influencers are extremely powerful when it comes to getting traffic into your restaurant. An influencer can have a million followers, but only have a couple of 1,000 followers engaging with their content. Worse, they can have a million followers and none of those followers are in your area. So, engagement is much more important than the amount of followers influencers have.

The next thing is social media marketing. Especially if you're trying to stay local or stay within 15 miles of your hotel. Social media marketing can be a powerful tool. The first thing I suggest trying is post swapping, which means I will swap posts with local businesses. I will post their business to my page and in return they will post my business to their page. This way, it costs us nothing to bring in customers for each other's business. Make sure that their business complements your business. For instance, if I don't sell ice cream, I will swap posts with the ice cream parlor because their business complements my business. After they finish eating in my restaurant, they can run and go get some ice cream.

The next best thing besides influence marketing and post swapping is going to be online ads. When you're running these types of ads I like to use placement campaigns and a lot of videos. Video gives people a visual sensation of how good the food is going to be. For food, I would go all out on this subject and hire a food photographer and a decent production team that can get the job done right.

Next thing I would do is photos; photos work very good for specials. Take a nice, beautiful picture, it's worth the price. Many people forget to put the original retail amount of that dish; make sure you captioning your photos in such a way as to capture as much profit as possible. If the original retail amount is $30 and you're selling it for $20, make sure you put the $30 there and cross it out so people know what the original price was. A lot of times a guest will see one price and think that's the price forever. If you're discounting an item, they know it's a temporary discount and may feel urgency to get it before the price goes back up.

The other thing that works very well is coupons, believe it or not. Coupons still exist and they're still going very strong. I still get circulars in the mail for McDonald's, Dunkin Donuts, and Hardee's. The reason why they keep putting these circulars in the mail is because they work. Everybody is looking for a deal. But not everybody is looking for a free meal. And if you have any celebrities visiting, make sure you take pictures with those celebrities and post them. I walked into one barbecue restaurant and an award-winning grill master had all types of celebrity pictures on the wall for guests to see who had eaten there before. That's great, but I would probably rather have that picture in an ad or on social media for guests to see so they know that these people are coming into this location. Make sure you take advantage of any type of celebrity publicity your restaurant can receive.

Driving Traffic To The Restaurant From The Room

Just having a menu inside guest rooms is not enough. If you want to stand out, if you really want to drive traffic from the room to the restaurant, you're going to have to put specials inside those rooms. Personally, I also suggest coupons in the rooms. Right next to the guest review card or next to the notepad I will put a $5 or $10 coupon for an appetizer or half price appetizer. When the guest gets inside the room, the first thing they want to do is go back downstairs to take advantage of the special or the coupon. Next, make sure you have commercials. A lot of hotels can show their own commercials inside of the room. You need to put those specials and those menu items inside those commercials on the preview channel. When they first turn on the TV, the first thing that they see is some food from the hotel restaurant.

Make sure pictures of your menu items are displayed everywhere because you're going to need four to six touches just to get the average person downstairs to a hotel restaurant. They're going to walk in, they're going to see the food at the front desk because you have a picture of the menu specials at the front desk. The front desk agent is going to tell them their favorite meal and point them in the direction of the restaurant. They get on the elevator; they see another sign for the restaurant. From the elevator they go to the room and turn on the TV, they see a commercial or some pictures of the food inside the restaurant. And then when they go to their nightstand, they see a coupon for that restaurant inside their room. That's five to six touches to bring that business downstairs.

Driving Local Traffic To The Restaurant

If you really want your restaurant to survive, it must have local traffic. The number one way to drive local traffic to the restaurant is to get local, get out there. Go out to association meetings, homeowners' association meetings and other gatherings. Don't be afraid to put together a platter and drop it off at an office building or at a warehouse or factory with menus. Host meet-ups in your restaurant during low traffic hours. In addition, you must take advantage of major holidays like Valentine's Day, Fourth of July, and offer packages.

Especially if you're a full-service hotel, you should offer a rate package with breakfast, lunch, or dinner included. This works very well with corporate guests that don't get reimbursed for food through their company. If they select a rate that includes a meal, they get a free meal and full reimbursement for the stay from their company. Finally, make sure you have food and wine tastings, tappa style. This works very well when you're trying to target previous guests to get them back in the door.

Conclusion

Generating more revenue does take a little more work, but it pays off in the end once you get the systems in place. Expenses are always going to be there, but revenue will come and go if you allow it. Don't allow it or worse, try to do everything by yourself. If you need help, reach out to me or one of the other contributing authors in this book. We are always here to help you when you need it.

Now you have the tools to take control of your property, the tools to climb the STR report to its highest point, and the tools to change your career and financial situation.

Don't waste them because revenue waits for no one! Get Going!

Acknowledgments

I would like to acknowledge the following.

1. My wife for making this possible and always supporting me. I love you very much.
2. My mentors Craig Sullivan and Glenn Haussman, for always helping whenever I needed good advice. They are the best mentor anyone can have.
3. Special shout out to Russell Edmond, better known as Russell of Hotels for keeping us motivated everyday with his podcast.
4. My friend Peter Wenzell from Wenzell and Fisher Hospitality who always have the best hotel task force staff and always looks out for me no matter what.
5. Special thanks to Dr. Jeffrey O for being a true pioneer in our industry.
6. Carita Montgomery, my self-publishing book coach for getting me to the finish line.

About The Authors

Contributing Author Craig Carbonniere Jr

Craig Carbonniere Jr is a hotel industry veteran and Certified Hospitality Digital Marketer (CHDM). He implements marketing strategies to achieve revenue growth and return on investment (ROI) for his lodging clients. Before becoming an award-winning supplier, he spent a decade managing various hospitality disciplines for Grand Pacific Resorts, Interstate Hotels & Resorts, Starwood Hotels & Resorts, and The Walt Disney Company.

Craig is an accomplished speaker who regularly facilitates digital marketing educational sessions for hospitality associations such as California Hotel & Lodging Association (CH&LA) and AAHOA. He also serves as Vice President of Marketing on the Board of Directors for Hospitality Sales & Marketing Association International (HSMAI).

Craig earned the award as one of the Top 25 Extraordinary Minds in Hospitality Sales, Marketing, and Revenue Optimization and is a trusted advisor for developing hotel e-commerce strategies.

Contributing Author Doug Kennedy

Doug Kennedy, founder and President of the Kennedy Training Network, Inc, based in Davie, FL, has been a fixture on the hotel and lodging industry's conference circuit for over three decades, having spoken at hundreds of associations, brand, and management company conference events.

Over 40,000 hoteliers have participated in small group training workshops he has presented personally throughout North America and in places like Sao Paulo, Singapore, Kaula Lumpur, Malaysia, Sophia, Bulgaria, Moscow, Russia, Florence, Frankfurt, Milan, and Amsterdam.

Thousands of others worldwide read his monthly training articles in publications such as HotelNewsNow, HotelMarketing.com, Hotel Online, VRM Intel, Hotel News Resource, VRMA Arrivals, Hotelier Maldives, STAAH Blog, and 4Hoteliers.

During his career Doug has founded three companies, starting with Check-Inn Training in 1989, HSA International which he co-founded and operated from 1991-2003, and his current company, Kennedy Training Network (KTN), which he started in 2006.

KTN specializes in training for: Hotel sales, hospitality and guest service staff, front desk, and reservations sales. Training is offered in traditional formats, live virtual webcam training, and online (self-paced) eLearning.

KTN also provides telephone mystery shopping, and remote call scoring assessment of real call recordings.

Contributing Author Halee Whiting

Halee Whiting is a creative, outside-of-the-box, seasoned hospitality professional that offers a different perspective on sales, marketing and content creation. She decided to create Hospitality with a Flair because helping hotels is her passion. After an extensive work history with various brands and independent hotels on property and in a remote capacity she knew with that hotels could be serviced and helped better.

The mission of Hospitality with a Flair is to create custom sales approaches for hotels. A one size fits all hotel sales support service does not work for every property. Halee's approach is to work together with hotel owners to create a service plan with them that will strengthen the hotel's personal brand, create elevated experiences for the hotel's guests and increase revenue!

Prior to founding Hospitality with a Flair, Halee has worked in the hospitality industry for 16+ years. She started in housekeeping and at the front desk. From there she soared into Sales & Catering by force in many different managerial roles. Her most recent role prior included being a Regional Director of Sales over a portfolio of up to 13+ hotels from independents to various brands like Hilton, Choice, IHG, Wyndham, GrandStay and Red Lion. Halee also has experience with Casino Hotels, Radisson and Best Western. She has also served as the youngest Hotel Executive Committee Chair for her local CVB and even chaired her own committee that specialized in Travel/Tour/FIT destination sales. When she doesn't have her hands in hotel work, she is writing for her own travel blog and keeping up with her busy family.

Contributing Author Deborah Gardner, CMP, CVP

Better known as the "Triple Threat," Deborah's multifaceted expertise as a meeting/event professional, hotel supplier, and dynamic professional speaker, elevates her presence in the fiercely competitive world of performance and entrepreneurship.

With three thriving businesses and a reputation as an energetic keynote speaker, emcee, podcaster, and six-time bestseller, Deborah's accomplishments include attaining the highest esteemed Certified Meeting Professional (CMP) Emeritus status, a testament to her 30+ years of exemplary service in the hospitality profession.

As one of the first female sports broadcasters in radio and television for major networks like CBS and NBC, Deborah is an ultimate hype woman and energy shifter that brings a unique perspective to mega international stages. As a pro athlete, she infuses her presentations with firsthand experiences and proven cutting-edge research, turbocharging teams, leaders, and audiences such as, Walmart, Fairmont Hotels & Resorts, Intel, Siemens, Best Western International Hotels, Event Service Professionals Assn., Florida Apartment Assn., Fox Restaurants, Teneo Hospitality Group and more.

As the creator and host of the highly acclaimed hospitality broadcast show, HOSPITALITY TODAY LIVE, Deborah takes pride in pioneering initiatives like the International Hospitality Women's Day and

International Hospitality Student's Day, further solidifying her status as a trailblazer in the industry.

Other recent honors include Top Hospitality Guru, Meetings Today Magazine Top 20 Meetings Trendsetters, Smart Meetings Magazine's Top 50 Smart Women Leaders, Meetings Mean Business Ambassador, Fabulous Arizona Magazine's Fabulous People to Watch, crowned as Mrs. Arizona 2020/2021 and Mrs. America with the American Queen Organization 2021/2022.

Off duty, Deborah lives in Phoenix, swimming or hanging out with her hubby and their furry rambunctious lover-boy, Bear.

For more information or to contact Deborah Today:

Deborah Gardner, CMP, CVP
DG INTERNATIONAL, LLC
www.DeborahGardner.com
Deborah@DeborahGardner.com
623-341-9077 (Cell)

Contributing Author Calvin Tilokee

An abundance of creativity married with the analytical skills developed as an experienced Director of Revenue led Calvin to create Revpar Media LLC in 2020.

Revpar Media focuses on helping hospitality businesses take a strategic approach to their social media. Through creative storytelling, Revpar Media helps businesses create authentic engagement with their audience. Authentic engagement is key to building an audience that will convert to paying guests. Calvin has personally built large followings across memes, travel and self-development brands. As someone who is an influencer in his own right, Calvin provides proven methods of growth to Revpar Media's clients.

Author Bruce Jordan the Michael Jordan of Hotels

Bruce Jordan is the Managing Partner of Hotel Guest Management. He oversees product development, revenue generation, and marketing. He is a hotel revenue expert and specializes in reviving failing and under-performing hotel assets.

Bruce Jordan is former IHG Corporate and has over 20 years of hotel experience working for the top brands and franchises including Wyndham, Marriott, IHG, Hyatt, Hilton, and more. He has managed over 30 hotels and overseen 3 hotel renovations. He has managed over 1 billion dollars in assets and over 300 million dollars in revenue.

Bruce was given the herculean task of saving one of the worst hotels in Kissimmee Florida. A 400-room hotel that was infested with drugs and prostitution and was facing foreclosure. In 5 month, Bruce Jordan turned around the hotel taking it from a 2.8 to a 3.8 review score and taking the revenue numbers from $60,000 and to over $300,000 a month. Saving the hotel from foreclosure. After this impossible rescue, Mr. Jordan was bestowed with the title of "Michael Jordan (MJ) of Hotels".

He is also the host of the hit award winning hotel competition review show Hotel Management Do's and Don'ts, the Hotel Insider and True Hotel Leaders which is one of the top 30 Podcasts for 2021, 2022, and 2023. Mr. Jordan is one of top 25 Social Media Influencers for 2021,

2022 and 2023. In addition, he's also one of the top 50 Most Powerful People in USA Hospitality for 2021, 2022 and 2023 and the top 2024 Notable Leaders according to the International Hospitality Institute.

You can reach Bruce Jordan at hotelrevenuebible.com

Or by contacting

BAJ Publishing and Media LLC
P.O. Box 781108
Orlando, Florida 32878

Other Hotel Books Available by
BAJ Publishing and Media

A new addition comes out every year.
Visit frontdesklog.com for more information.

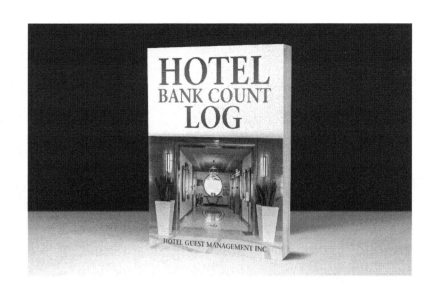

Available at:
BestHotelBooks.com

BEST HOTEL BOOKS

Available at:
BestHotelBooks.com

NOTES